THE DRY FLY AND FAST WATER

THE
DRY FLY
AND
FAST WATER

BY GEORGE M. L. LA BRANCHE

A MASTER'S ADVICE ON FISHING THE DRY FLY

THE DERRYDALE PRESS

LANHAM AND NEW YORK

THE DERRYDALE PRESS

Published in the United States of America
by The Derrydale Press
4501 Forbes Blvd., #200, Lanham, Maryland 20706

Distributed by NATIONAL BOOK NETWORK, INC.

First Derrydale paperback printing 2000

ISBN 978-1-56833-156-0 (pbk.: alkpaper)
Library of Congress Card Number: 00-102293

PREFACE

To expound a theory into willing ears upon a trout stream is one thing; to put those same ideas into writing so that they may be intelligently conveyed to one who reads them is quite a different thing. Of this I am convinced. However this may be, my readiness to do the one induced in some of my angling friends the belief that I could do the other. They insisted that I try—and this book is the result. My experience in preparing these pages has filled me with the profoundest respect for those persons who may be truthfully characterised as authors. I began the work with a good deal of timidity, and, as it now appears to me, considerable temerity. After completing the task to the best of my ability I submitted the manuscript to some of my credulous friends. Strange to say, after reading it, even then they insisted that I publish it. By this decision it seems to me they proved two things—their friendship for me and their absolute unfitness to be literary critics.

Even so, under their instruction and guidance, the book is presented to the angling public with the hope that it may find some small favour among them.

G. M. L. L.

May, 1914.

CONTENTS

THE DRY FLY AND FAST WATER

THE DRY FLY AND FAST WATER

CHAPTER I

EARLY EXPERIENCES

FROM my earliest boyhood I have been devoted to the fly fisher's art, having been in-
ducted into it by my father, who was an ardent
angler before me. For more than twenty years
I have fished the near-by streams of New York
and Pennsylvania; not a season has passed
without having brought to me the pleasure of
casting a fly over their waters. Each recurring
year I find myself, as the season approaches,
eagerly looking forward to the bright days when
I can again go upon the streams. In the early
days of the season, however, I am content to
overhaul my gear, to dream alone, or talk with
others about the active days to come; for I
have never enjoyed going upon the waters so
long as the air still holds chill winter's bite.

During the early years of my angling I fished

my flies wet or sunk. Such was the manner universally prevailing upon our streams and the manner of my teaching. I had read about the dry fly and knew that its use was general in England, which country may justly be said to be its place of origin. That this is true may not be gainsaid, yet it seems to me remarkable that with all the reputed ingenuity of Americans the present development of dry fly fishing for trout should be almost entirely the work of British sportsmen. That the use of the dry fly on streams in this country has not been more common may be due to a pardonable disinclination upon the part of expert wet fly anglers to admit the weakness of their method under conditions as they now exist. Their method has served them well, as it did their fathers before them, and perhaps they are loath to surrender it for something new. In the earlier days trout were much more abundant in our streams, and the men who fished the streams and wrote upon the subject of fly fishing in this country may have felt that a knowledge of the habits and haunts of the fish was more essential to success in taking them than the employment of any particular method. The merits of up-stream over down-stream fishing caused some discussion among anglers, and some of these discussions found permanent place in angling literature. The discussion, however, seems always to have been confined to the question of position and seems never to have been extended to the manner of fishing the flies. Individual characteristics or experiences led some to advocate a certain manner of manipulating the dropper-fly and others to recommend the sinking of the tail-fly to a greater depth; but the flies seem always to have been manipulated upon the theory that to be effective they must be constantly in motion. It seems to have been conceded by all that the flies should be always under the control and subject to the direction of the rod, thus enabling the angler to simulate living insects by twitching them over or under the surface of the water—a practice that is the exact opposite of the method of the dry fly fisher, who casts a single fly lightly upon the surface of the water and permits it to float with the current over or near the spot where he knows or believes a fish to lie.

Many expert wet fly anglers in this country have been using the floating fly for years, but most of them use it only on water where they consider it may prove more effective than the wet fly—usually upon the quiet surface of a pool or on flat, slow water. Contrary to the prevailing notion, however, the floating fly is not a whit more deadly on water of this character than the wet fly, when the latter is properly fished. The difficulty in taking trout on such water may be ascribed to two causes: (1) When the water is low and clear, or where it has little motion and the surface is unruffled, the fish is likely to perceive the activities of the angler at a greater distance than is possible in rougher water, and is thus sooner warned of his approach. (2) When the angler has been careful to conceal himself from the fish, the fly cast in the usual wet fly manner is likely to be refused because of its unnatural action, the wake made by dragging the flies across the smooth surface being sufficient at times to deter even small fish from becoming interested in it. The floating fly is far more effective than the wet, "jerky" fly, because, as no motion is imparted to it, it is more lifelike in appearance. When such a fly, properly presented, is refused such refusal may be due as much to a disinclination upon the part of the fish to feed as to his suspicion having been aroused. The wet fly fished *sunk*, with no more motion given to it than is given to the floating one (a single fly being used in each case), will prove quite as deadly as the latter on smooth water; and where many casts with the dry fly may be necessary to induce a rise, the sunk fly may appeal upon the first or second attempt, because its taking demands of the fish no particular exertion. The effort of the angler to impart a "lifelike" motion to the wet fly upon the surface will often be quite enough in itself to defeat his purpose. Such effort should never be made on clear, glassy water, for, while it may occasionally be successful, unseen fish are put down.

For many years I was one of those who firmly believed that only the smooth, slow stretches of a stream could be fished successfully with the dry fly. Experience, however, has taught me that the floater, skilfully handled, is applicable to any part of a swift stream short of a perpendicular waterfall. My unorthodox method of using it—which may be described as creating a whole family of flies instead of imitating an individual member thereof—may be characterised by some as "hammering" or "flogging," and condemned as tending to make fish shy because the leader is shown so often. My answer to this is that if the blows struck by the fly are light no harm is done. And, further-more, if showing gut to the fish really tends to make them more wary, the sport of taking them, in my estimation, is pushed up a peg.

It is not my purpose to contend that the dry fly is more effective than the wet fly, although I do believe that, under certain conditions, the dry fly will take fish that may not be taken in any other manner. I do contend, however, that a greater fascination attends its use. All game birds are pursued with the same weapon, but the more difficult birds to kill have the greater attraction for sportsmen; and my pre-dilection for the dry fly is based on the same principle.

My first dry fly was cast over the Junction Pool—the meeting of the waters of the Wil-lowemoc and the Mongaup—about fifteen years ago, and the fact that I cast it at all was due more to the exigency of the occasion than to any predevised plan for attempting the feat. Every day in the late afternoon or evening I noted four or five fish rising in the pool formed by these two streams, and repeated attempts upon my part to take one of them by the old method absolutely failed me, although I put forth diligent efforts. The desire to take one of these fish became an obsession, and their constant rising to everything but my flies exasperated me to the point of wishing that I might bring myself to the use of dynamite.

One evening in looking through my fly book I found in one of the pockets a clipping from the *Fishing Gazette*, which I had placed there during the preceding winter. If my memory serves me, I think this article was entitled "Casting to Rising Fish." At any rate, the caption was such that it caught my eye, as it seemed to suggest the remedy for which I was searching. The article proved to be an account of the experience of an angler who used the dry fly for trout, and his exposition of the manner of using it seemed so clear that I determined to try it myself upon the pool over the rising fish in the late afternoon. Barring my inability to execute properly the things the author described and that I was called upon to do, the only stumbling-block in my way was the impossibility of my obtaining an artificial fly that resembled the insects upon which the trout were feeding, and the author laid a great deal of stress upon the necessity of using such an imitation. I remember that, in a measure, I was mildly glad of this, because I felt that I

would have an excuse for failure if I were unsuccessful. I "doctored" some wet flies into
what I thought to be a fair imitation of the dry
fly by tying the wings forward so that they
stood at right angles to the body, and then
sallied forth to the pool. On my way to the
stream I went alternately hot and cold betwixt
hope and fear. I rehearsed in my mind all the
things I had to do, and I think I was coldest
when I thought of having to float the fly. The
writer had recommended the use of paraffin-oil
as an aid to buoyancy, and this commodity was
about as easily procurable in Sullivan County
at that time as the philosopher's stone; in my
then frame of mind the latter would probably
have proven quite as good a buoyant. The pool
was but a stone's throw from the house, and I
arrived there in a few minutes, only to find a
boy disturbing the water by dredging it with a
worm. Him I lured away with a cake of choco-
late, sat down to wait for the rise which came
on shortly, and by the time I was ready there
were a half dozen good fish feeding on the surface. I observed two or three sorts of flies
about and on the water, to none of which my
poor, mussed-up Queen-of-the-Waters bore the
slightest resemblance. This did not deter me,

however, and I waded boldly out to a position some forty feet below and to the right of the pool. My first cast amazed me. The fly alighted as gently as a natural insect upon the surface, and, watching it as it floated down toward the spot where a fish had been rising, I saw it disappear, a little bubble being left in its place. Instinctively I struck, and to my astonishment found that I was fast in a solid fish that leaped clear of the water. The leaping of this fish was a new experience, as I had never seen a trout jump as cleanly from the water. After a few flights and a determined rush or two I netted him—a rainbow trout just over a foot long and the first I had ever taken. This variety of trout had been placed in the stream a few years before as an experiment, and few had been caught. Stowing my prize in my creel, I prepared for another attempt as soon as the excitement in the pool had subsided. The fly I had used was bedraggled and slimy and would not float, so I knotted on another. My second attempt was as successful as the first, and I finally netted, after a tussle, a beautiful native trout that weighed a little over one pound. Four fine fish fell to my rod that evening, all within half an hour, and the fly was taken on the first cast each time. If such had not been the case I doubt very much if I should have succeeded, because I am certain that my confidence in the method would have been much weakened had I failed to take the first fish, and my subsequent attempts might not have been made at all, or, if made, would probably have ended in failure.

For several years after my first experience with the floating fly I used it in conjunction with the wet fly, and until I read Mr. Halford's "Dry Fly Fishing," when, recognising his great authority and feeling that the last word had been said upon the subject, I used the dry fly only on such water as I felt he would approve of and fished only rising fish. Some time later on I read George A. B. Dewar's "Book of the Dry Fly." Mr. Dewar says: "I shall endeavour to prove in the course of this volume that the dry fly is never an affectation, save when resorted to in the case of brawling, impetuous streams of mountainous districts, where it is practically impossible of application." Here again I felt inclined to listen to the voice of authority and felt that I must abandon the dry fly. I was accustomed to fish such streams as the Beaverkill, Neversink, Willowemoc, and

Esopus, in New York; the Brodhead and Sho-
hola, in Pennsylvania; the Saco and its tribu-
taries, in New Hampshire, and others of similar
character—all brawling, impetuous, tumbling
streams—and it seemed to me that by continuing to use the dry fly on them I was profaning
the creed of authority and inviting the wrath
of his gods upon my head. Since then, however, I have continued the use of the dry fly
on all of these streams, and a number of years
ago abandoned the use of the wet fly for all
time.

Since I began casting the fly over the streams
of the region I have mentioned their character
has greatly changed in many particulars, and
conditions are not the same as they were twenty
years ago. The natural streams themselves
have changed; the condition of the water flowing in them has changed; the sorts of fish in-
habiting the waters have changed; and the
methods of taking the fish have changed, or
should change; and it is to show why this last
is true that the following pages are written.

The changes that have taken place in the
character of our mountain streams may be attributed to many causes, chief of which, however, is the destruction of the timber which at

one time covered the hills through which they
have their course.   During the frequent and
long-continued droughts the denuded hills, baked
hard as rock, shed the occasional summer showers
as readily as the back of the proverbial duck;
the streams become turbid torrents for a few
hours, after which they run down, seemingly to
a lower mark than before.   So long as the forests
covered the watersheds the rains as they fell
were soaked up by the loose and porous earth
about the roots of the trees, were cooled in the
shade of the leaves and branches, and slowly
percolated into the tiny brooklets through
which they were fed to the streams for many
days.   Under present conditions the temperature of the streams is much higher than formerly, and, while the temperature has seldom
risen to a point where it has been fatal to the
fish, it has risen in many streams to a point
that is distasteful to the native brook-trout
(*Salvelinus fontinalis*).

It is not unreasonable to assume that the
heat of the water has a very deleterious effect
upon the vitality of the fish during certain
years when the droughts are long sustained
and, should the condition have existed for a
great length of time prior to the spawning sea-

son, that the progeny for the year would probably come into being lacking the vitality necessary to overcome the attacks of natural enemies and disease. A bad spawning season, of
course, reduces the hatch for the year, but is
ordinarily not noticed by the angler until two
or three years later, at which time the unusu-
ally small number of immature fish taken becomes a matter of comment among the fre-
quenters of the streams. A native angler who
has made it a practice to visit the spawning-
grounds of trout for over twenty-five years stated
to me that during the season of 1910 the redds
were occupied by trout, but that not a fish
spawned on any of them in a stretch of nearly
a mile of the stream which flows past his home
and which was under his constant observation
during the entire season. It is difficult for me
to believe that such a thing could have been
possible, yet I know the man to be a careful
and accurate observer, and his statement must
be given credence. He seemed frightened at
the prospect and alarmed as to the future of
the stream, and he besought me for an explanation of the condition—which I was unable to
give. My diary for that year had been destroyed, so that I was then, and am now, unable

to even theorise as to whether or not the failure
to spawn was due to weather conditions prevailing at that time. Let us hope, assuming
that my informant was not mistaken, that the
curious condition observed by him was confined
to the stretch of the stream that he investigated.
Let us hope, further, that the fish, even in that
stream, will not become addicted to such an
ungenerous and unnatural habit.

Great numbers of trout must be destroyed in
the periodical freshets that carry masses of ice
tearing and grinding over the beds of the mountain streams. When the ice breaks up gradually
there is very little danger to the fish; but a
sudden and continued thaw, accompanied by a
steady fall of warm rain, washes the snow from
the hillsides, swells the streams into wild torrents, and rips the very bottom out of them.
Any one who has witnessed the forming of an
ice-jam and its final breaking must marvel at
the possibility of any fish or other living thing
in its path escaping destruction, so tremendous
is the upheaval. A few years ago a jam and
freshet on the Brodhead, besides uprooting
great trees along the banks, lifted three iron
bridges within as many miles from their stone
abutments and carried each of them a hundred

yards down-stream, leaving them, finally, mere masses of twisted iron. These bridges were twelve or fifteen feet above the normal flow of the stream, yet, even so, they did not escape destruction. How, then, is it possible for stream life to stand against such catastrophe? Furthermore, this scouring of the beds of the streams by ice and debris carried down during the floods undoubtedly destroys great quantities of the larvæ of the aquatic insects which form an important part of the trout's food, and this, too, indirectly affects the supply of fish available to the angler's rod. After a severe winter and a torrential spring there is a noticeable dearth of fly upon the water—another of the many causes of lament of the fly fisherman of to-day.

Directly or indirectly, all of the conditions above described are the result of the ruthless cutting of the timber from the hills. Happily, there is reason to hope that these conditions are not going to grow worse, because the present movement toward the preservation of the forests seems to be gaining headway; conservation of nature's resources will come to be a fixed policy of our National and State Governments, and if the policy is pushed with vigour and persistence our children's children may some day see our old familiar streams again singing gaily through great woods like those our fathers knew.

With the elements, man, beast, and bird all intent upon its destruction, it is a marvel that our native brook-trout survives. But live on he does, though his numbers constantly decrease. The great gaps left in his ranks are being filled by the alien brown trout—his equal in every respect but that of beauty. True, there is a wide difference of opinion in this particular, and there are some who will go so far as to say that the brown trout is, all round, the better fish for the angler. When feeding he takes the fly quite as freely as the native trout, leaps vigorously when hooked, grows rapidly to a large size, and seems better able to withstand abnormal changes in the temperature of the water, which are so often fatal to *fontinalis*. No one deplores the scarcity of our own beautiful fish more than I do; but we must not be blind to the facts that the brown trout is a game-fish, that he is in our streams and there to stay, and that our streams are suited to him. He is a fish of moods and often seems less willing to feed than the native trout; but for that reason alone, if for no other, I would consider him the sportier fish. When both varieties are taking

freely and their fighting qualities compared, it
is not easy to decide which is the gamer. The
leaping of the brown trout is often more im-
pressive than the determined resistance of the
native trout, and the taking of a particularly
active or particularly sluggish fish of either
variety is frequently made the basis for an
opinion. It seems to me that, in any event, the
taking of even a single fair fish of either variety
on the fly is an achievement to be put down as
a distinct credit to the angler's skill and something to be proud of and to remember. Our
native brook-trout is much loved of man. It
has come to be something more than a fish:
it is an ideal. It will always hold first place in
the hearts of many anglers. I fear, however,
that it must yield first place in the streams to
its European contemporary, he having been
endowed by nature with a constitution fitted to
contend against existing conditions and survive.

My many years' experience upon the streams
of New York and Pennsylvania have brought
me to realise that changed conditions call for
an expertness of skill and knowledge that
anglers of the past generation did very well
without. The streams now are smaller, the fish

in them fewer and warier, and the difficulties of the angler who would take them greater. Three flies fished down-stream may still be a permissible method for those who pursue the trout of the wilderness, but the sportsman should now be willing to adopt the use of the single light surface fly when pursuing the trout of our domestic waters; and, if he does adopt it, as he gains in skill he will come at last to realise that it has a virtue not possessed by its wet brother. I can illustrate my point best by quoting an experience of my own that happened several years ago.

One day, while fishing an up-State stream, I met a dear old clergyman, who, after watching me for a long time, came up and said: "Young man, I have fished this stream for nearly forty years, and they will tell you at the house that I have been accounted as good as any man who ever fished here with a fly. I have killed some fine fish, too; but in all that time I have never been able to take trout as regularly as you have taken them in the few days you have been here. I am told that you use the dry fly and have some particular patterns. If it is not asking too much, will you be good enough to give me their names and

tell me where they may be obtained?" I gave
him the information he asked, and volunteered
some instruction by pointing out that his gear
was not suitable for the work, convincing him
that such was the case by placing my own rod
in his hands. We sat in the shade for a couple
of hours exchanging ideas, and to prove or
explode a theory of mine he agreed to fish a
certain pool with me later in the day. He used
my rod and rose and killed a brown trout of
one pound five ounces, a little later leaving the
fly in a heavier fish. He was an expert at placing the fly, but, not being used to the stiffer
rod and lighter gut, he struck too hard, with the
resultant smash. Being a good angler, he easily
overcame this difficulty. He now fishes only
with a rod of fine action and power, which enables him to place his fly easily, delicately, and
accurately a greater distance than was possible
with the "weeping" rod he formerly used.
This he abandoned once and for all, and with it
the wet fly. He came into the knowledge and
enjoyment of the dry fly method, and he has
since then frankly admitted to me that he
greatly regretted having realised so late in life
that the actual taking of trout constitutes but
a very small part of the joy of fly fishing.

CHAPTER II

THE VALUE OF OBSERVATION

SEVERAL years ago I was looking on at a tennis match between the champion of America and one of the best men England ever sent to this country, and as I watched their play I could not help but marvel at the accuracy with which the players placed their shots. Their drives were wonderful for direction and speed. On nearly every return the ball barely cleared the net and was seldom more than a few inches above the top as it passed over. A friend who knew many of the experts told me how they attained to their remarkable precision. It was the custom of many of them, he said, when preparing for the big matches, to practise for accuracy by driving the ball against a wall. He said this was particularly true of the American champion, and that it was not unusual for him to use up a dozen or more balls in a day's practice. The wall had painted across its face a line of contrasting colour at a height from the ground equivalent to that of the top of a regulation tennis net, and upon the line were painted a number of disks about ten inches in diameter. Standing at a distance from the wall equivalent to the distance of the base-line of a regulation tennis-court from the net, the player would return the ball on its rebound from the wall, striving each time to so place it that it would strike just above the line. The accomplishment of a satisfactory score after a succession of drives would convince the player that he had good control of his stroke, and he would then turn his attention to the disks, against each of which he would drive twenty or more shots, taking them in turn and keeping a record of hits in each case. The accuracy developed by such practice was truly remarkable, and I hesitate to mention the number of times in succession one expert made clean hits—it seemed an incredible number.

I have seen golfers practising the weak places in their game for hours with as much zeal and earnestness as if they were playing a match, and a polo player of my acquaintance practises his strokes upon a field at his home, riding his ponies as daringly and recklessly as though a championship depended upon his efforts. The devotees of these and similar active sports are keenly alive to the necessity of constant practice, that spirit of competition which is so much a part of them making any endeavour that will aid toward high efficiency, or improve game or form, seem worth while. And in all sports, particularly those in which the competition is individual, whenever and wherever opportunity presents itself there will be found hundreds of enthusiasts following every play of the expert, keenly studying his method, observing his form, and absorbing and storing the knowledge so gained for their own practice later on court or field. So, too, even though competition has no place in fly fishing, and should have none, the angler ought to strive always to "play a good game." He should practise the tactics of his art with the same zeal as do the followers of competitive sports if he hopes ever to become an expert fly fisherman in the highest sense of that much misused term.

The casual angler who looks upon fishing as merely incidental to his periods of recreation, during which his chief concern is the recuperation of tired brain and unstrung nerves, may feel that he is making a business of his pleasure by devoting much time to the study of his angling. In a measure, this is true, and it would

be asking much, indeed, of him who thinks of
fly fishing only as a pastime. But to him who
realises that it is a sport—a sport that is also
an art—there is no incident, complex or simple,
that is unworthy of his attention and consideration. No sport affords a greater field for observation and study than fly fishing, and it is
the close attention paid to the minor happenings
upon the stream that marks the finished angler.
The careless angler frequently overlooks incidents, or looks upon them as merely trivial,
from which he might learn much if he would but
realise their meaning at the time.

Of greatest importance to the dry fly angler
is that mastery of the rod and line that enables
him to place his fly lightly and accurately upon
the water. I venture to assert that one who
has had the advantage of expert instruction in
handling a rod, and is thereby qualified to deliver a fly properly, will raise more trout upon his
first attempt at fishing a stream than another
who, though he knows thoroughly the haunts
and habits of the fish, casts indifferently. The
contrast between the instructed novice and the
uninstructed veteran would be particularly noticeable were they to cast together over the
same water in which fish were rising freely.

Whether or not the novice would take more fish than the veteran is another question. Lacking experience, the novice would probably hook few fish and land fewer. But he would be starting right, and the necessity of overcoming later on that bad form likely to be acquired by all who begin without competent instruction would be eliminated, and the stream knowledge of the veteran would come to him in time.

The beginner should watch the expert at work and should study particularly the action of the rod. He should note that the power which impels the line forward starts from the butt, travels the entire length of the rod, is applied by a slight forward push rather than by a long sweep, and ends in a distinct snap. He will soon learn that the wrist must do the real work, and no better scheme for teaching this has ever been devised than the time-honoured one of holding a fly book or a stone between the casting arm and the body. The proper action of the rod will be best learned if he fasten that part of the butt below the reel to the forearm with a piece of string, a strap of leather, or a stout rubber band, the effect of which device will be to stop the rod in an almost perpendicular position when the line is retrieved. The pull of the line as it straightens out behind him will be distinctly felt, will give him a good idea of the power and action of his rod, and serve as a signal for the forward cast. He should practise casting as often as his spare time will allow—over water when possible, but over grass if necessary. He should not wait until the stream is reached and actual fishing problems begin to press upon his notice for solution. His mind will then be occupied with many other things; hence, the knack of handling the rod should have been already acquired.

After the beginner is satisfied that he can properly place and deliver his fly he should turn his attention to the study of the fish and the currents of the stream. If he has been a wet fly angler his experiences will stand him in good stead, as it will qualify him to locate the likely haunts of the fish. Long and varied though his experience may have been, however, the use of the dry fly will open avenues of observation and knowledge that were hidden from him while he practised the old method. My own experience is responsible for this rather broad statement, but not until after I had become an ardent advocate of the dry fly, and had abandoned the wet fly for good and all, did I realise the truth of it. In the beginning I was ever on the alert for rising fish, and, instead of boldly assailing promising water, wasted much time, on many occasions, scrutinising the water for some indication that a fish was feeding. In this way I frequently discovered non-feeding fish lying in places where I had not expected to find them. Such fish were then the more easily approached because I was able to assume a position myself that would not disclose my presence. Just as frequently, too, I have seen fine fish cruising about, and have taken many that might have been driven away by the slightest movement on my part. In many cases I have been compelled to remain absolutely motionless for ten or fifteen minutes before a fish would come to rest long enough to make worth while an attempt to get a fly to it. Nearly every time, too, that a fish has been hooked I have seen it actually take the fly—an action always instructive, because fish vary greatly in their manner of taking, and interesting, because in it lies one of the real charms of fly fishing.

The continued use of a floating fly upon water where the angler sees no indication of feeding fish, but where experience tells him that they may lie, seems to develop in him a remarkable keenness of vision. This is a direct result, perhaps, of the attention which he gives to his fly. My own experience is that while I am watching my fly float down-stream some stone of irregular formation, peculiar colour, or difference in size from others about it, lying upon the bottom, arrests my eye, with the effect of making the water appear shallower or clearer than it really is. My fly appears to be the centre of a small area upon the surface of the water through which everything is seen as clearly as through a water-glass, the shadow of the fly itself upon the bottom often being plainly discernible. Anglers who fish the dry fly learn to identify the living shadow that appears suddenly under the fly as a trout ready to take it on its next drift down-stream, and to recognise a fish as it sidles out from the bank or swings uncertainly toward the fly just as it passes the boulder that shelters him. In either case an interesting opportunity is afforded, particularly for exercising a very necessary attribute—self-control.

It may be that many happenings I now see upon the stream passed unnoticed when I used the wet fly because of some lack of concen-

tration and observation. If this be so, I have
the newer method to thank for the development
of those faculties. I have learned not to overlook a single minor happening. Perhaps my
keenness to ascribe some meaning to the slightest incident has resulted in the building of many
very fine structures of theory and dogma upon
poor foundations. This may be true, but I am
certain that their weaknesses have always become apparent to me in time; and, on the other
hand, I am just as certain that I have been
greatly benefited by my habit of close attention
to the little things that happen on the stream.
For instance, I cherished the belief for many
years that one advantage of up-stream fishing
lay in the fact that when the fly was taken the
hook was driven into the fish's mouth instead
of being pulled away, as in down-stream fishing.
I thought this to be one of the strongest argu-
ments in favour of up-stream fishing, and, theo-
retically, it is. But I know now that many
fish that take a floating fly do so when they
are headed down-stream. While there are still
many reasons why up-stream fishing is the better
method, this particular argument no longer has
weight with me.

As I remember it, the strongest admonition

of my early schooling on the stream was never to remain long in one place. I was taught to believe that if a rise was not effected on the first few casts subsequent effort on that water was wasted—that the trout would take the fly at once or not at all. I clung to this belief for years, until one day I saw a fine fish lying in shallow water and took him after casting a dozen or more times. Since then I have taken fish after upward of fifty casts, and I rarely abandon an attempt for one that I can see if I feel certain that it has not discovered me. Even when I have not actually seen a fish, but have known or believed one to be lying near by, the practice has proven effective. Thus I have had the satisfaction of accomplishing a thing once believed to be impossible; but I have gained more than that: I have learned to be persevering and, what is still more important, deliberate. The man who hurries through a trout stream defeats himself. Not only does he take few fish but he has no time for observation, and his experience is likely to be of little value to him.

The beginner must learn to look with eyes that see. Occurrences of apparently little importance at the moment may, after considera-

tion, assume proportions of great value. The
taking of an insect, for instance, may mean
nothing more than a rising trout; but the position occupied by this fish may indicate the
position taken by others in similar water. The
flash of a trout, changing his position preparatory to investigating the angler's fly, will frequently disclose the spot occupied by him before
he changed his position; and, later on, when the
fish are not in the keenest mood for feeding, a
fly presented there accurately may bring a rise.
The quick dart up-stream of a small trout from
the tail of a pool is a pretty fair indication that
a large fish occupies the deeper water above;
it indicates just as certainly, however, that the
angler has little chance of taking him, the excitement of the smaller fish having probably
been communicated to his big relative.

The backwater formed by a swift current on
the up-stream side of a boulder is a favourite
lurking-place of brown trout. I was fishing
such places one day, and found the trout occupying them and in rather a taking mood.
In approaching a boulder which looked particularly inviting, and while preparing to deliver my
fly, I was amazed to see the tail and half the
body of a fine trout out of the water at the side

of the rock. For a moment I could not believe that I had seen a fish—the movement was so deliberate—and I came to the conclusion that it was fancy or that a water-snake, gliding across the stream, had shown itself. Almost immediately, however, I saw the flash of a trout as he left the backwater and dashed pell-mell into the swift water at the side of the boulder. Down-stream he came until he was eight or ten feet below the rock, when, turning sharply and rising to the surface, he took from it some insect that I could not see. Up-stream again he went, and shortly resumed his position in the dead water, showing half his body as he stemmed the current at the side of the rock. Once more this performance was repeated, and I knew I had stumbled upon an interesting experience. Hastily measuring the distance, hoping to get my fly to him before some natural insect might excite him to give another exhibition of gymnastic feeding, I dropped it about three feet above him, and, contrary to my usual method of retrieving it as it floated past the up-stream side of the boulder, I permitted it to come down riding the top of the wave, when the same flash came as the trout dashed after it. The fish could be plainly seen almost directly under the fly. As it reached the rapidly flattening water below the rock, he turned and took it viciously, immediately darting up-stream again. He was soundly hooked, however, and I netted a fine fish lacking one ounce of being a pound and a half. My experience heretofore had been that if a fly were placed a yard or so above this point and allowed to float down to the rock a feeding fish would rush forward—often as much as two feet—and take it, immediately turning or backing into his position again. I had assumed from this observation that when the fly passed the rock or backwater without a rise it should be retrieved and another try made. This fish satisfied me, however, that when really feeding, or when inclined to feed, trout may be lured comparatively long distances by inviting looking morsels. Either he did not decide to take the fly until just as it was passing him or else he liked the exercise of the chase. In any event, he was not peculiar in his habit, because four more fish were taken in the same manner the same day.

In most cases when the fly is cast above a boulder lying in swift water (which I consider, under certain conditions, one of the best places to look for brown trout) it will be taken as it approaches the rock, the trout darting out and retiring immediately to avoid being caught in the swifter water on either side of his stronghold. But if it is not taken, and is permitted to float down with the current, it may bring a response.

It was a somewhat similar observation which prompted the practice and, I must say, rather dubious development of what some of my friends are pleased to call the "fluttering" or "bounce" cast. This cast is supposed to represent the action of a fluttering insect, the fly merely alighting upon the water, rising, alighting again, repeating the movement three or four times at most; finally coming to rest and being allowed to float down-stream. It rarely comes off, but when it does it is deadly; and, for the good of the sport, I am glad that it is difficult, though sorry, too, for the pleasure of accomplishing it successfully is really greater than that of taking fish with it. The cast is made with a very short line—never over twenty-five feet—and the fly alone touches the water. The action of the fly is very similar to that produced by the method known as "dapping," but instead of being merely dangled from the rod, as is the case when "dapping," the fly is actually cast.

It should be permitted to float as far as it will after its fluttering or skipping has ceased. The beginner practising the cast will do well to cast at right angles to the current, and he should choose rather fast water for his experimenting. The speed of the water will cause the fly to jump, and the action it should have will be the more readily simulated than if the first attempts are made on slow water.

I had made a flying trip to the Brodhead, and, with that strange fatality which seems so often to attend the unfortunate angler rushing off for a week-end in the early season, found the stream abnormally high and horrible weather prevailing. After many attempts to get into the stream, with results equally disastrous to my clothing and temper, I abandoned all idea of wading and walked and crawled along the bank, casting my fly wherever I could but rarely finding good water that could be reached, and rising but a few small fish. As there was a gale blowing in my face directly down-stream, it was practically impossible to place a fly where I wished with any delicacy, and I decided to abandon the sport after trying a pool just above me that I knew contained big fish. My first cast on this water, made during a lull, fell lightly, but brought no response, and after a further half dozen fruitless attempts I began to think of the fine log fire at the house. I made one more cast, however, this time in the teeth of the wind. Using but twenty-five feet of line and a short leader, I was able to straighten both in the air. The wind kept all suspended for an instant, the fly, accompanied by a small part of the leader, finally falling upon the water, where it remained but a fraction of a second, the wind whisking it off and laying it down a foot away. This happened five or six times as the fly came down-stream, and during the time it was travelling a distance of not over eight or ten feet five trout, each apparently over a pound in weight, rose to it, but missed because it was plucked away by the wind just in time to save them. I did not get one of them, and, as it was practically impossible to continue casting under the prevailing conditions, I left the stream. It was brought home solidly to me that day, however, that it was the *action* of the fly alone that moved the fish—and my day was not badly spent. I cannot say as much of the many other days since then that I have spent in what I feel were rather foolish attempts to imitate the effect produced by the wind on that day.

The study of the positions taken by big fish when they are feeding, and those which they occupy when they are not, is an important part of the education of the fly fisher. Each time the angler takes a good fish or sees one feeding, if he will note in his diary its position, the condition of the water, temperature, atmosphere, time of day, and the insect being taken, he will soon have an accumulation of data from which he may learn how to plan a campaign against particular fish at other times. Extremely interesting in itself, the study of insects is of great value to the angler in his attempts at imitation, and the information gleaned from autopsy might not be acquired in any other manner.

It may be said to be an axiom of the fly fisher that where a small trout is seen feeding rarely need a large one be looked for. But the actions of a small fish in sight may sometimes indicate the presence of a larger one unseen. The taking of a fine trout on a certain stream in Sullivan County, on August 27, 1906, after one of those long periods of drought so common in recent years, convinced me of this. I had been waiting for even a slight fall of rain, and, quite a heavy shower having come up the evening before, I started for this stream. Upon my arrival there I was surprised to learn that not a drop of rain had fallen in weeks, and that the shower which had been heavy twenty miles away had not reached the vicinity. While driving from the station to the house at which I was to stop, along a road that paralleled the stream, the many glimpses I had of the latter filled me with misgivings. At one point the stream and road are very near each other, and, stopping my driver, I got out to look at a famous pool below a dam which had long outlived its usefulness. It was a sizzling-hot day, and at that time—eleven o'clock—the sun was almost directly overhead; yet in the crystal-clear water of this pool, with not a particle of shade to cover him, lay a native trout fourteen inches in length which afterward proved to weigh one pound three ounces. Too fine a fish, I thought, as I clambered back into the carriage, to be occupying such a place in broad daylight, and I promised myself to try for him later in the afternoon. Returning about six o'clock, I found him in the same position, and during the full twenty minutes I watched him, while he appeared to be nervously alert, he never moved. Notwithstanding the fact that everything was against me, and knowing that the chances were more than even that the fish would see me, my rod, or my line, I made my plans for approaching him; yet, busy as I was, I could not rid my mind of this ever-recurring thought: with all the known aversion of his kind to heat, and their love of dark nooks, why was this fish out in this place on such a day? Why did he not find a place under the cool shade of the dam? With the instinct strong within him to protect himself by hiding, the impulse must have been much stronger that forced him to take so conspicuous a stand—a mark to the animals which prey upon his kind. As there were absolutely no insects upon the water, and scarcely enough current to bring food of other sort to him, he could not have been feeding. The only reason, then, to account for his being there—the thought struck me forcibly enough—was his fear of a bigger fish. The logical conclusion was that if a fish of his inches (no mean adversary) exposed himself so recklessly the one that bullied him must be quite solid. I tested this fellow's appetite with a small, pinkish-bodied fly of my own invention, and, standing about forty feet below and considerably to the left, dropped it three or four feet above him; but, although it was certain he could see the fly, he made no attempt to go forward and take it. As it neared him, however, he rushed excitedly to the right and then to the left, taking the fly as it came directly over him, and, before I could realise what had happened, came down-stream toward me at a great rate. As he was securely hooked, I kept him coming, and netted him quietly at the lip of the pool.

That this fish did not take the fly the instant it fell meant to me that he was afraid to go forward into the deeper water which harboured his larger fellow; and his action as the fly appeared over him meant that, while he wanted it badly enough, he would not risk an altercation with the other, which might also have seen it. When he did finally decide that the coast was clear, he took it quickly and rushed down toward the shallower water where he might be secure against sudden attack.

If some of the theories developed in those few moments appear fanciful, it must be remembered that my mind was occupied with the thought that the pool contained a larger fish, and the conclusions based upon the subsequent actions of this smaller one only tended to strengthen this belief. Fanciful or not, I was rewarded a few minutes later by the sight of a monster tail breaking the surface just under the water that trickled over the apron of the dam. Having prepared a gossamer leader, preferring to risk a smash to not getting a rise, I dropped a small Silver Sedge—which I used because it could be more plainly kept in sight— almost immediately in the swirl and was at once fast in a lusty fish. After many abortive attempts to lead him into the diminutive net I had with me, I flung the thing, in disgust, into the woods. I finally beached the fish and lifted him out in my hand. He was a fine brown trout, eighteen and three quarter inches in length, and weighed, the next morning, two pounds nine ounces.

While I was engaged with this fish another rose in practically the same spot under the apron of the dam. Hurriedly replacing the bedraggled fly with a new one, I waited for the trout to show himself, which he did presently, and again I was fast—this time in one of the best fish I have ever seen in these waters. It seemed an interminable length of time, though probably not over ten minutes, that I was engaged with this one, and it was impossible to move him; he kept alternately boring in toward the dam and sulking. In one of the latter fits I urged him toward me somewhat too strongly, and he was off. Immediately I was afforded a sight of what I had lost as he leaped clear of the water in an evident endeavour to dislodge the thing that had fastened to his jaw. The smash made as he struck the water still resounds in my ear, and when I say that this fish would have gone close to five pounds I but exercise the right to that license accorded all anglers who attempt to describe the size of the big ones that get away. Having one good fish in my creel, however, I really had some basis for my calculation—at any rate, he was one of the best fish I have ever risen. Examining my leader, I found it had not broken, but the telltale curl at the end proved that, in the fast-gathering gloom, I had been careless in knotting on the fly.

CHAPTER III

THE RISE

ANY disturbance of the surface made by a trout is usually referred to as a "rise," but the characterisation is erroneous except where it is applied to fish feeding upon the surface. Rising fish are the delight of the dry fly fisher, but are really the easiest fish to take—provided, always, that no error is made in the presentation of the fly. The angler is called upon to exhibit a fine skill in casting, a knowledge of the insect upon which the fish is feeding, and to make the proper selection of an imitation; but he is aided materially by being apprised of the location of the fish, and is further helped by the knowledge that he is throwing to a willing one.

The study of the habits of rising fish, or, to use a more inclusive term, feeding fish—because a feeding fish may not be a rising one—is of the utmost importance to the dry fly enthusiast, who knows how difficult it is to induce a fish feeding on or near the bottom to rise to his floater.

Inasmuch as the principal literature available on this delightful branch of angling is the work of Englishmen who have, with unfailing unanimity, used the same terms in describing the positions and actions of feeding fish, it would be unwise to attempt to employ others, and for that reason I have made use of them throughout this chapter.

Compared with our swift-flowing waters, the gentle, slow-moving, chalk streams of Southern England offer greater advantages to students of the habits of feeding fish, not only because of the greater deliberation with which the trout secures his food in them but also because a greater number of aquatic insects contribute to his sustenance there than are found on our swift streams; consequently, the English student has far greater opportunity for observation. The water-weeds grow so heavily on these English streams that at times it is found necessary to cut them out to some extent if fly fishing is to be pursued. These weeds harbour great numbers of snails, shrimps, larvæ, etc., of which the trout are inordinately fond, and when the fish are seeking this luscious fare the trials of the angler fishing with a floating fly are, indeed, many. Trout feeding in this manner are de-

scribed as "tailing" fish, from the fact that the
tail of the fish is observed breaking the surface
of the water violently or gently, as the case may
demand, in his efforts to secure or dislodge his
prey. Heavy weed growth being unusual on
our swift streams, the trout do not have the
same opportunity to feed in the manner described as their English cousins, and, consequently, the American fly fisherman is not particularly interested in tailing fish; but it must
not be forgotten that caddis larvæ abound in
our waters, and that trout occasionally pick up
crawfish, snails, and other *Crustacea* and *Mol-
lusca* from the bottom, usually in the less rapid
parts of the stream. Fish so feeding do break
the surface with their tails, and, even though
the tail be not actually seen, the action of this
fin in maintaining the fish's equilibrium causes
a swirl which is often mistaken for a rise. A
trout often shows his tail in rapid water but
this is occasioned by the necessity of forcing
his head down to overcome the force of the
current after he has taken food of some sort
upon the surface or just below it, and the action
must not be confused with that of a fish feeding
upon the bottom in the more quiet stretches.

The term "bulging" is applied to fish that

are feeding below the surface upon the nymphæ
of insects about to undergo the metamorphosis
which produces the winged fly. The trout is a
very busy fellow at this time, and covers left,
centre, and right field with equal facility; but
he occasionally misses, and at the instant of
his viciously breaking the surface of the water
the insect may be seen taking its laboured flight
—escaping by a hair's breadth the death which
pursued it. When trout are feeding in this
manner the angler's patience is taxed to the
utmost, and after a succession of flies has been
tried without success the discomfited angler
may be excused if he concludes that his artificial is not a good imitation. He may not be
far wrong.

Although aside from the main subject of dry
fly fishing, I will in this connection attempt to
show how the sunk fly may be used successfully
against the "bulger." As the nymph is still
enclosed in its shuck, or case, it is quite obvious
that an artificial fly made with wings is not
an imitation of it. Consequently, a hackle-fly
should be used even though it, too, is a poor
imitation. A suggestion of the general hue of
the natural is quite sufficient. The cast is
made some distance above the feeding fish, so

that the fly will approach the trout approximately as the nymph would, *i. e.*, under water and rising. If no attempt be made to impart motion the fly drifting with the current will be more natural in its action than the angler can hope to make it appear by manipulation. Besides, the trout is an excellent judge of pace, and, making for a natural looking morsel, is sorely disappointed and not likely to come again if it is jerked away from him at the moment he is about to take it. One fly only should be used, and quite as much care is required in its delivery as would be necessary were a floating fly being presented. Errors made in casting are more readily concealed by the current in the case of the sunk fly.

When the attention of the fish is fixed upon insects beneath the surface it is difficult to attract his notice to a floating fly, except, perhaps, at such times as the fly appears before him when he is close to the surface; but it can be done—and in two ways. Fish so feeding are moving about, darting here and there taking nymphæ. A swirl made by the fish in all likelihood only marks the place where he was, and he may be a yard or more up-stream, or to right or left, where he went to secure the nymph. If

the swirl is made by his tail at the time he
starts for the insect and not at the moment
he takes it, there is little knowledge as to his
actual position to be gained from the disturbance; the only indication is that he is feeding.
The angler must be able to distinguish between
the disturbance made by a bulger feeding under
water and that made by a fish taking a winged
insect upon the surface—often not a very difficult thing to do—and he must conduct his campaign accordingly. The signs of the surface-
feeding fish are easily discernible to the quick
eye. The gentle rise in slow water, or the
swifter rush where the fly is in the current,
starts a ripple immediately from the centre
made by the nose or mouth of the fish, and, of
course, is unmistakable where the actual taking
of the insect is seen. In all cases the surface is
broken. The commotion made by the bulging
fish is started under water, and, while the disturbance is ultimately seen upon the surface,
the form it assumes is more of a swirl or boil
and is quite unlike the concentric rings that
mark the actual breaking of the surface.

Occasionally, as I have said, the "fielder muffs
the fly," and this is the moment that, if the
angler be alert, an artificial fly dropped im-

mediately over the fish is likely to meet with a hearty welcome. I am convinced that a trout that misses his prey in this manner frequently stays on the spot where he lost it long enough to give the angler an opportunity to present his fly, if he is within striking distance—and ready. He must be prompt in making his throw, however, because the fish may have his attention attracted elsewhere at any moment. If a rise be not effected at once the angler should not try again immediately, because the possibility of the fish having left his position, or of having been scared by the line, or of frightening another which may have come between, is too great to make the attempt worth while.

When fish are feeding all over the pool, and the angler is impatient and not content to stand idly by waiting for an opportunity such as described, let him try the following method: He should look the water over carefully, keep out of it if possible, and choose the spot where the fly is to be placed. Knowledge of the water and of the habits of the fish will guide him in this choice, but he should not cast to the swirl. Having chosen his water, which should be toward the head of the pool, not much above its centre, and preferably where the current will carry the fly down faster than the leader (the choice being governed naturally by the character of the stretch), he should place his fly some distance—a yard or two—ahead of the swirl and a foot or two to the side nearest him, allowing it to float down eight or ten feet; if no rise is effected he should place his fly in the same spot again and again until he has made twenty-five casts or more. It is important that each cast should be executed with the same precision and delicacy as marked the first attempt.

The method is based upon the theory that a feeding trout—or even one that is not feeding, for that matter—may be induced to take up a position in line with the direction in which the angler's fly is travelling, under the belief that flies are coming down-stream in such quantities as to make them worth investigating. Once this position is compelled it is only a question of time and patience upon the part of the angler. The trout will rise eventually to one of this "hatch." The angler cannot hope to have this *coup* come off, however, if he has made any mistake in his casting or has shown himself or his rod.

The beginner practising the method will

find it most difficult to restrain an almost un-
controllable impulse to leave off casting in
the one spot in order to place his fly over the
swirl made by some other fish. If he gives
way to that impulse he courts failure—and
down comes the house he is building. It is
quite likely that a trout is preparing to investi-
gate the "hatch" at the very moment the angler
changes his water, and, of course, will be frightened away by seeing the rod or the line which
is thrown over it to the other fish. The method
usually employed by the novice is productive of
nothing. Because many feeding fish are seen,
he hurriedly casts over this one, then over that
one, in the hope that his fly will be taken, and
finally gives up in despair when his hope is not
realised.

If a mistake unfortunately occurs—the danger of which naturally increases in proportion
to the number of casts made—it is quite useless
to carry the attempt further. The angler should
retire for a few moments or continue a bit farther up or down stream, selecting a spot some
distance from where he began, and always
bearing in mind the necessity for throwing
above and to the near side of the swirl. If no
mistake is made the chances are at least even

that those early evening "rises" which have so long mocked his skill may show a profit. The angler, however, may spend a profitable quarter hour watching the insects upon the water or rising from it, and catching some for closer examination. During this time, if there is a cessation of swirls, as there likely will be, it indicates that the nymphæ are becoming fewer and that, the "hatch" being over for the present, his last chance has come for a try at the bulgers. He should proceed, as before, to create his artificial "hatch," and he will have even a better chance of success because the attention of the trout will be less occupied.

In selecting water in which to place the fly, in order to take bulging fish by the method I have suggested, the angler will do well to choose that where the current is swift but the surface unbroken; and too much stress cannot be laid upon the importance of having the fly float down as nearly as possible in the same lane and position each time. When the trout have ceased feeding upon the nymphæ his opportunity for casting to fish that are really rising is come, and he may try these until darkness drives him home.

One who has observed trout feeding upon the tiny *Diptera* called indiscriminately by anglers "black gnats," "punkies," "midges," etc., is quite inclined to believe that, while "smutting" is rather an inelegant term to apply to the fish, the insects themselves, considering the provocation, have been let off too lightly in being described as "smuts" and "curses." These diminutive pests seem to be abroad at all times of the day, but are particularly numerous in the late afternoon, when clouds of them may be seen hovering over the still water of the pools. At such times the trout seem to be busily feeding, but the keenest observation does not disclose what it is they are taking. These "curses" are so small that it seems incredible that large trout should be interested in them. That they are is easily proven by autopsy, and I have found solid masses of them in the gullets and stomachs of sizable fish, proving that they must have been extremely busy if the insects were taken singly. If one could see these tiny things upon the water, and could see a trout rise to them, he would have convincing evidence that they are taken singly; but, though my eyesight is still good, I have never been able to satisfy myself that I have actually seen a fish take one of them. After many experiences with trout under such conditions, and particularly after a series of observations extending on one occasion over a period of four successive days, I am almost ready to believe that the fish do not wait for them to fall upon the water. This notion—perhaps fanciful—came to me while on a pool that had been my objective during an afternoon's fishing, and upon which I intended to close the day. Arriving there about a half hour before sundown, I was not a little delighted to find fish rising freely all over. After studying them for a few moments I concluded that they were not "bulging," because the surface was broken each time with a distinct "smack." They could not have been "tailing," because the water was about four feet deep. They were not rising to any insects that I could see, although I looked long and steadily. Yet they rose freely, and each fish rose again and again in practically the same spot.

Using the smallest fly that I had with me, a flat-winged "black gnat" tied on a No. 16 hook, I cast faithfully but unavailingly for some time, endeavouring to interest two fish which were nearest me, and until I was quite ready to confess myself beaten. However, I decided to try them with a larger fly, and while preparing to tie this on my attention was attracted by four

distinct clouds of insects hovering over the water
—on the wing, certainly, but making no flight.
They were merely dancing in the air about two
feet above the pool. Watching closely, I saw the
insects gradually decrease this distance until but
an inch or two separated the lower extremity of
a cloud of them from the water, when directly
underneath would come another "smack" as
the tail of a trout broke the surface. Immediately the swarm would scatter, though but for
an instant, collecting again to perform the same
evolution as before, when again they would be
scattered by a fish under them. This happened
to all four swarms in rapid succession, and it
was quite evident that a trout was under each.
Every time the insects were close to the water
the tail of a trout would be seen and water
would be thrown amongst them. Query: Did
the trout deliberately throw water at these
insects with the intention of drenching those
within reach and in order that they might be
picked up at leisure after they had fallen into
the stream? And, if so, why were the fish not
observed in the act of picking them up? Or
did the sight of the insects excite the anger of
the fish, or a sport-loving instinct—if, indeed,
fish are capable of these emotions?

My subsequent experience with these fish tended only to confuse me further in my guessing. This "spattering" game went on for fifteen or twenty minutes, and was brought to a conclusion, finally, by the retirement of the "curses," which left the scene perpendicularly, going straight up until lost to view. After they had disappeared the fish stopped rising. Having marked them down, I determined to have one more try with a large fly, and, to my amazement, my first cast brought a swift rise, but no connection was made. Resting the fish for a moment, I tried him again; he rose, and I was fast in what appeared to be a very good fish. I had great difficulty in leading him to the lower end of the pool, so that I might not disturb the others, and finally netted him. He proved to be a small trout and was hooked on the side just above the tail. I then tried the others, and, although I rose each one at least three times, I hooked none, nor on any occasion did I feel that the fly had been touched. By this time it was quite dark and I left for home.

On the three following days I met with the same experience. I had innumerable rises to my fly after the "curses" had left, hooked but one fish each evening, and, by a remarkable coincidence, each foul and near the tail. Again, query: Was this mere accident or were the trout trying to drench my fly? Were they still on the lookout for the sport afforded them by the clouds of insects? The gullets of the fish taken were lined with the small insects, the stomachs also being well filled with them; but how the fish took them after they had risen without my seeing some indication of it, I cannot imagine. I feel quite certain that they were not taken at the instant of the rise, because the insects did not touch the water at any time; nor did the trout show any part of their bodies above the surface except their tails. So they could not have been taken in the air. Some day, perhaps, the problem may be solved, but at present I have no solution to offer.

A bulging or smutting fish and a cursing angler are not a rare combination. If there is anything more perplexing and vexing than the sight of fish rising all about and one's best efforts going unrewarded, I cannot imagine what it is.

A bulging fish may be taken with an imitation of the insects he is feeding upon, either sunk in one form or floating in another; but a smutting fish cannot be appealed to with any imitation

of his food of the moment. The colour of
the pests may be imitated, but no ingenuity
of man can fashion an artificial so that it will
resemble in size the minute form of the natural;
and, even if ingenuity could do it, the hook to
be used in conformity would be absolutely useless and probably quite as difficult to make as
the fly. Lacking a correct imitation of the
"curses," which, even if good, might not be
taken, one may accept the rebuffs offered to
his fly with an equanimity born of the knowledge that he is not alone in his trouble.

If smutting fish are to be taken at all they
will probably be taken on a fly that has no resemblance to any particular insect except, perhaps, one that is indigenous to the stream, or
one in which the angler has faith. It may assume any form, flat-winged or erect. Colour,
of course, is not important, except that it should
not be too brilliant; a fly of sombre hue, such
as the Whirling Dun, Cahill, or Evening Dun,
being very effective, the Gold-Ribbed Hare's Ear
or Wickham's Fancy frequently being accepted.
I am inclined to think that a small fly receives
no more attention than a large one, if as much;
but nothing larger than a No. 12 or No. 14 hook
should be used.

Meeting with failure while the insects are about, the angler should rest until they have disappeared and then, having marked the position of the fish, try them with the method described for bulgers. Failing again, let him figure it out if he can.

When fish are feeding upon some particular species of insect it is quite logical to assume that an imitation of that species will appeal to them more readily than an imitation of any other. But when the insects are numerous, as they are on occasions, and the fish are moving about, the chance of the artificial fly being selected from among the great number of naturals upon the water is one to whatever the number may be. As a general rule, the larger fish take up positions which by virtue of might are theirs for the choosing and almost invariably in places where many flies are carried down by the current. If they be rising steadily the angler is enabled to reduce the odds against him by his ability to place his fly near the spot where he knows one to be lying. It does not follow, however, that because certain insects are observed flying about they are of the species with which the trout are engaged for the moment.

If an insect be observed flying as though

it had some objective point in view, it may
be safely concluded that it has but recently
assumed the winged state. In this case it is
attractive to the fish only at the moment it
emerges from its shuck, or immediately afterward while it is resting upon the water, for the
very obvious reason that it does not appear
upon the water again until it is about to deposit
its eggs, if a female, or, if of the opposite sex,
when it falls lifeless after the fulfilment of its
natural duties.

When the insects are seen dancing about over
the water, oftentimes a considerable height
above it—in some cases thirty feet or more—
the observer may be quite satisfied that they
are the perfect males of the species waiting for
the females to appear. After the sexual function has been completed the female may be seen
flitting over the water, dipping to the surface
and rising again, in the act of depositing her
eggs, finally coming to rest as the function is
completed, only to be swept away to her death.
As she does not travel any considerable distance
during this last act of her life, she proves of
greatest interest to the fish at this stage of it.

One who observes closely will see that at the
moment the female approaches the water, or

during her subsequent dips, attempts, frequently successful, are made by the fish to capture her. As these efforts require some activity, they are resorted to usually by the more agile dandiprats. The larger fish are quite as interested in the dainty morsel as are their younger brothers, but they do not make the same frantic efforts to secure it, preferring to attend the fly closely in its movements until the opportunity presents itself to take it with little or no exertion. This is usually at the time ovipositing is about completed or the fly is resting upon the surface of the water preparatory to another flight. The females of some species are less active in the performance of this duty than those of others. They select the more placid stretches of the stream, ride quietly upon its surface, and the eggs exude from the oviduct as they sail along. Occasionally, after travelling in this manner for a time, they rise from the water, fly a short distance, and settle again. They are incapable of guiding themselves and are naturally carried along by the current and over the fish.

It has been my observation that during the period of ovipositing a great majority of the insects are headed directly up-stream, instinctively knowing, perhaps, that contact with the current in that position will more readily relieve them of their burdens. And, while I have no certain knowledge that it is so, I am inclined to believe that the setæ or hair-like tail enables them to assume and maintain this position. At any rate, it should be the angler's ambition to imitate this action, and present his counterfeit with its tail or hook end coming down to the fish. This gives the added advantage of having the business end taken first and eliminates the danger of disturbing the fish by having the shadow of the leader thrown over him in advance. To do it successfully calls for a nicety of judgment in the handling of rod and line; but when the skill is acquired its successful execution has its own reward.

The utmost caution should be used in approaching a feeding fish. The danger of putting him down does not depend solely upon his getting sight of the angler; he may also be apprised of the angler's coming by the excited darting up-stream of smaller fish which have been below him. If the character of the water to be fished indicates that other and smaller fish may be hidden, or if their presence be disclosed by *their* feeding, it is much safer to cast at right angles to the selected fish than to attempt to cast from below and over the smaller ones. If the situation demands that the fly be placed from this position it should be floated down to the fish from a point two or three feet above and should not be cast directly over him. Inasmuch as the trout is more likely to see the rod at this angle, a longer line should be thrown than would otherwise be necessary and, if the fish has been well spotted, great care must be exercised in presenting the fly without undue accompaniment of leader.

The fly may be presented alone by using the horizontal cast. If an attempt is being made to drop the fly three feet above the fish, it is necessary to aim at a spot six feet above, with a bit longer line than will just reach, suddenly checking the cast at the very end as it straightens. This will have the effect of throwing the fly down-stream. The leader will describe a sharp curve and follow after, and will not be seen by the fish before he sees the fly. After the fly has alighted, the rod should be held consistently pointed directly at the fly and in a horizontal position. Held in this way, it is less likely to be seen by the fish and a better control of the line is had if a rise be effected.

There are, in fact, good reasons why the rod should be held horizontally whenever and wherever the floating fly is being used, the line being stripped in by the unoccupied hand as much as may be necessary to keep the fly under control.

If the current be rapid between the angler and the fish, he should use a foot or two more of line and try to throw a larger curve in the leader so that the fly may reach the fish before drag is exerted upon it. If the cast be well done there is at least an even chance that the fly will be taken; if not well done, no move should be made to retrieve the fly until it has floated some distance below the fish, and even then the retrieve should not be made directly from the water with the full length of line. The line, leader, and fly will be swept down-stream at a speed depending upon the current, and will be approaching the angler's bank. By stripping the line in slowly and carefully, the fly may be lightly whisked off with little or no disturbance of the surface when there is little but the leader upon the water, and another attempt made. The angler may continue this process as long as he feels he has made no mistake.

If the fly has been refused after a number of casts, and the fish continues to rise, it is some

consolation to know that he has not been disturbed by the casting.   A change of tactics is
very often effective in such cases; and, if the fly
be placed very close to the fish instead of being
floated down to him, its sudden appearance,
giving but little time for investigation, may
cause him to rise to it.

When a rising fish may be cast to without
disturbing those below him, the angler is in a
more favourable position.   Where practicable,
the effort should be to make the throw with
the leader curved and above the fly.   Naturally, this is more easily accomplished when the
fish—looking up-stream—is on the angler's left
hand.   Unless one be ambidextrous, or skilful
enough to throw with the right hand from over
the left shoulder, a fish under the right-hand
bank is difficult to reach in this manner.   Until
the cast has been mastered, no attempt should
be made to throw the curve; but one need not
despair of taking fish in this position, even
though this skill be lacking.   The fly may be
thrown straight, but from a more obtuse angle;
and if, instead of being placed directly over or
above the fish, it be placed slightly above and
a foot to the near side of the spot where he
rose, the danger of scaring him off with the

leader is lessened, and the chance of his taking it not a bit.

Where a long cast is required, the line should never be extended to the length required to reach the fish. The distance should be measured carefully, and, when the fly in the false or air casts reaches a point five or six feet from the fish, that much line—which should be stripped from the reel and held in the left hand—should be allowed to pass through the guides on the next forward cast. This is called shooting the line. Not only is it of great assistance in attaining accuracy, but the momentum imparted to the "live" line, that part already clear of the top, is lost and does not travel down to the fly, which, shorn of impulse, remains suspended for an instant above the water and falls thereon as lightly as the proverbial feather.

The fly should never be aimed directly at the water, but at an imaginary point three or four feet above, and a like distance in advance of, the spot it is desired to reach. This direction must be implicitly observed in this method of casting, because the fly will invariably fall short unless a greater length of line be used than is apparently necessary. Very often the fly will fall heavily if just the required length of line is used without "shooting."

Where a fish is rising in the strong current, a short line, not over twenty-five feet, will be sufficient and quite enough to handle, as it is returned very quickly to the angler. In this case the "shoot" may be abandoned in the actual delivery of the fly and used only to lengthen the line between casts after the retrieve, which should be made only when the fly has passed considerably behind the fish—the exact distance naturally being determined by the circumstances. The line should be stripped with the left hand to keep pace with the speed with which the fly travels and no faster, else its action will not be natural. Nothing but the fly and leader should be on the water, and as little of the latter as possible. Get behind the fish, but do not cast directly over him. The fly should come down past him to one side or the other, with the leader always on the same side—away from the fish.

Early in the season, if the weather be propitious and the stream in good condition, it is not unlikely that fish will be seen rising throughout the day—perhaps not all of the time but often enough to keep the angler alert. The fact that they are rising at all is quite sufficient to arouse his interest, because, even though the fish nearest him does not take his fly, the one above may; and, all things considered, he may hope to have a fairly interesting day, with the further chance, if fortune smiles, of a good one.

How different the situation confronting the angler who elects to fish the streams in the hot summer months, with the water at its lowest mark, clear as crystal—or gin, as the Englishman has it—and not a fish to be seen rising the whole livelong day, for the very good reason that no insects are about to offer inducement. Even in June these conditions sometimes prevail, with the redeeming feature, however, that toward evening the falling temperature, or the approach of darkness, or both, seem to induce a rise of insects, with an accompanying rise of trout. The angler, having patiently waited for this time, sets hard at work and is content to take a couple of fair fish in the hour or so before dark.

I confess to a certain weakness for the stream during those periods of extreme heat when the local experts agree that it is almost impossible to take fish. Actuated, perhaps, as much by a desire to take a good fish as by the hope of learning whether or not their theories were correct, I have gone to the stream under such conditions and have had some curious experiences. I have taken fine fish on broiling hot days when there seemed to be little difference between the temperature of the water and the air. On days when the "hatch" has been so thin that one would be warranted in thinking that the trout had forgotten that there ever was such a thing as a fly, I have taken some of my best fish. On the other hand, there have been many occasions when I have met with utter defeat, and, all in all, I hardly know what I have really learned from the experiences, so varied have they been.

One insufferably hot July day convinced me, however, that there are times when trout are interested neither in food nor in anything else. For three sultry hours I cast over every likely spot. I never rose a fish. I never saw one rise. I did not see a fish.

At a beautiful pool, small but of good depth, considering the state of the water, I felt that my last chance had come, and, after covering the whole surface carefully, without result, deliberately waded into it, hoping to scare any fish that might be there and so learn where they were hiding. I did not see a fin, and had about decided it was tenantless, when, looking down, I saw, close to my feet, the tail of a fish sticking out from under a small boulder. I looked under the up-stream side of the boulder, hoping to see the fish's head, but could not, as there was no hollow on that side. I gently stroked that part of the fish in sight with the tip of my rod, and received in acknowledgment a gentle waving of the tail. Placing my gear behind me in the dry bed of the stream, I proceeded to move the boulder to see what manner of trout this might be. Not until I had it completely removed did he stir—and then he moved but a short distance to a similar hiding-place. He was a brown trout about fifteen inches long, and so sluggish was he that it would have been the simplest matter to have seized him with my hands.

A short distance above the pool there is a dam famous for the big trout which make their home under it. I covered the water faithfully, without success, and, after I had finished, crawled out upon the apron of the dam. Peering into the pool below, I saw, directly underneath me, eighteen or twenty trout ranging from six inches in length to one old "lunker" over twenty. As this spot had been cast over repeatedly, and apparently without any glaring error, I felt in no humour to try again, but determined to test their appetites in another way. Catching a half dozen grasshoppers, I dropped one in front of the big fish that led the school. He paid not the slightest attention to it. Neither did any of the others, not even the smallest one. I tried again, throwing another grasshopper a bit upstream so that it would float down in plain view for a longer time, and again provoked no interest upon the part of the fish. Finally, I killed one of the grasshoppers, crushing it so that it would sink, and threw it well above the fish. It came down under water directly on a line with the big fish, which deliberately moved a bit to one side, apparently to avoid having it touch him. Each fish behind him did the same thing, even the smallest ones ignoring it.

Now, what sort of a fly, wet, sunk, or dry, or, if the angler was inclined to try it, what sort of bait could he use to interest such fish? Under the conditions then prevailing—the thermometer recording 94 degrees in the shade, the stream at its lowest point, and the temperature of the water very high—I really believe that the only chance he might have had would have been with a very "wet" mint julep. Under the circumstances it would have required considerable self-denial to have offered that. This heat was exceptional, however, and fishing in such weather is quite as trying as fishing in the cold, blustering days of early spring. In either case, even if fish are taken, enthusiasm is not greatly aroused on the part of either angler or trout.

I confess I do not know what method of fly fishing one may use to entice a trout when the temperature is extreme, because when the fish is found under a boulder, as he probably will be, he will not see a floating fly, and it is almost hopeless to expect a sunken fly to attract any attention—witness the case of the idle fish and the grasshoppers. If fish not hiding in caverns refuse live grasshoppers dropped directly in front of their noses, it is quite evident that there is small chance of taking them on any sort of artificial lure.

Leaving out of consideration, however, the few periods of unbearable heat, that part of the season between June 15 and August 31 may have many days rich in experience for the angler, and even though there be many days when the fish will be found not to be rising to natural insects, the pleasure derivable from trying for success is commensurate with the difficulty of approaching and luring them.

When the streams are low and clear great circumspection and care are required in approaching fish or likely places and in presenting the fly. The slightest error will be detected at once, and subsequent attempts to interest the fish will be effort merely wasted.

The angler who carefully casts over and thoroughly fishes a likely piece of water should not come too quickly to the conclusion that it contains no fish. If it happens to be one of those days (too frequent in the experience of the present-day angler) when a great length of stream may be traversed without his seeing the slightest indication of a rising fish, he may, of course, if he be so inclined, comfort himself with the thought that the fish are not feeding and abandon his fishing. But I hope to show that upon just such days the proper use of the dry fly will measure the difference between an empty creel and some success, even though that success be limited to the probability of a single good fish.

An English dry fly angler fishing our Eastern American streams by rote and casting only over or to rising fish would have many empty days to record in his diary. Days and days might pass without his seeing the "dimple" of a big fish or even the splash of a small one, except, possibly, just at dusk; and at such times his skill and patience would be taxed as heavily as ever by any smutting fish of a chalk stream. But does it follow, as some authorities seem to have suggested, that because a fish is not risen by a few casts here and there it has no inclination to come to the surface or that such inclination may not be aroused? I think not, my experience having proven the contrary.

The entire theory of forcing the fish to rise to the fly is based upon the fact that a trout may be decoyed from the position occupied by it when not feeding to one fixed by the angler, provided, of course, the fish is not asked to come any great distance. The practice of the method necessitates considerable knowledge of the fish and of the character of the places it frequents. The fly cast, say, twenty times, in close proximity to the supposed lair of a fish, in nine cases out of ten will prove more effective than twice the same number of casts placed indiscriminately over the water. But no glaring mistake, such as undue splashing or frantic waving of the rod, is overlooked by the fish. If such errors have been committed, the angler had best retire and try some fish that has not become acquainted with him.

Having chosen the point of vantage from which to assail the fish, which choice should be governed, first, by reason of its being out of range of the trout's vision, and then by the availability of casting room behind—note the order of importance—the single fly should be placed a foot or two from the spot where the fish is supposed to be and to one side of it. The instructions given in regard to casting to bulging fish so as to produce the effect of a hatch should be followed to the letter. Even where the distance seems rather too far to expect the fish to travel, it is better to select water that flows continuously in one direction in which to place the fly. It is preferable to have the fly travel in one "lane" during its promenade, rather than to have its action marred by a possible drag resulting from an attempt to get it closer to the fish. If the fly has been natural in its action, it is quite likely that it has attracted the attention of the fish, and the angler may at any moment be amazed to see a trout backing slowly down-stream under it, seemingly coming from nowhere. This is the trying time, as the fish, having come closer to the angler, is more likely to be frightened off by any sudden movement; but if the angler is careful, the satisfaction of eventually seeing the fish rise deliberately and fasten to the fly is not to be measured by that of taking a larger fish by any other method.

Great care should be exercised in retrieving the fly from the water, because a fish taking up a position under the angler's lane of flies usually backs down-stream a bit. In no case should the fly be retrieved until it has floated down to a point nearly at right angles to or even below the rod. Strict observance of this rule will prevent scaring off many fish that might otherwise be induced to rise.

Where the swiftness of the current precludes any possibility of preventing drag, particularly in those miniature pools behind rocks in the centre of the stream called "pockets," the fly may be placed lightly thereon, and as lightly whisked away, being left but an instant, to be returned immediately and often, until the angler is satisfied that the pocket contains no fish, or that he is unable to interest them if it does. In any event, he need not feel that an opportunity has been lost to him because of his inability to avoid drag, for in this sort of water the error is not always observed by the fish.

There can be no question but that stalking a feeding fish and finally taking him on an artificial fly affords sport of the highest quality. The taking of a fish that may be seen but is not feeding, either because of lack of food or disinclination, is quite as difficult to accomplish, however, and is productive of equally good sport.

I relate the following story of the taking of a trout under almost impossible conditions, not so much to illustrate the success of the method as to show the satisfaction that attends the accomplishment of the feat. This individual fish is only one of many that I have taken similarly in the many years that I have fished with the floating fly, and the history of its taking is given here because it illustrates and bolsters up my claim that the dry fly repeatedly cast over a sluggish, non-feeding fish will induce him to rise.

The last two days of the season of 1909, August 29 and 30, found me on the banks of the Kaaterskill, at Palenville, Greene County, N. Y. This stream is a brawling one, resembling many Rocky Mountain streams, and some magnificent rainbow trout inhabit it; yet in six hours' fishing, one afternoon, I raised but one good-sized fish, in which I left my fly. The dozen or more fish from ten to twenty inches in length which could be seen restlessly swimming about in each of the pools appeared to be interested in nothing but a desire to escape the intense heat, and at length I abandoned the sport as hopeless.

A gentleman who had once lived in that section, and who had fished the streams of the surrounding country for over thirty years, invited me to fish a stream some miles away with him the next day. I accepted his invitation, and the morning found us on the banks of what should have been the Plattekill, but proved to be nothing but a mere trickle. With many misgivings I started in, my companion going upstream about a mile to fish down and meet me.

The only likely water within three or four hundred yards was a pool under a dam, and here I rose and pricked a good fish. Leaving him, I cut across a neck of land to meet my companion at the turn, and found him ready to quit. But I determined to try again for the fish I had risen, and, while following the stream back, discovered a pool against the bank, some eight

feet wide and not over a dozen in length, with
six feet of water in it. On the bottom lay a
fine brown trout, as motionless as if dead. He
was actually lying on the sand and pebbles,
apparently devoid of all interest in life. I with-
drew quietly and, getting below him and behind a tree-stump on the bank, put on a new
fly—a Whirling Dun—and, with but little hope,
sent the fly on its errand. It fell lightly upon
the glassy surface about a yard above the fish,
which was at all times in plain view; but he
seemed entirely oblivious to it. There was
practically no current to carry it down, and it
seemed an interminable length of time before
the fly got below the fish far enough for me to
take it off the water without disturbance; but
at last I retrieved it and, after drying it thoroughly, dropped it again. I repeated this opera-
tion six times before I noticed any change in
the position of the fish, and all of the time he
was just "lolling" on the bottom. The sixth
cast seemed to attract his attention, and, with
all fins moving, he lifted ever so little from the
bottom and stood poised. I felt that I had him
interested—that he was alert—and I knew that
the slightest mistake from then on meant failure,
complete and certain; and my excitement was

not helping a bit. Another cast, and I imagined I could see him tremble; at any rate, his fins moved rapidly, but without imparting any motion to the body, except to lift it an inch or two toward the surface. Each succeeding cast brought the same excited action of the fins and tempted him a few inches nearer the surface. I thought he never would reach the top, and felt that if he didn't get within his distance soon I would bungle the whole affair. At last, and after I had made more than twenty-five casts, he had risen to within six inches of the surface; as the fly was presented again, he made a determined rush, stopping just short of it and allowing it to float over him, apparently without further interest. I gently retrieved the fly, though I felt that it was all over, as the fish had probably detected the fraud. However, I made another cast and the fly fortunately alighted softly. The fish made the same rush, refusing it as before; but after the fly had floated down a foot or so, he turned slowly and deliberately down-stream, and, rising quietly, took the fly with a distinct "suck," turned to go down with it, and was fast.

This was not a very large trout—fifteen inches or so—but his taking afforded more genu-

ine sport than a dozen larger ones might have
yielded taken in any other way, because of the
circumstances under which it was accomplished.
I may have had a possible advantage over him,
because a floating fly had, probably, never been
cast on the stream before. Aside from this
fact, it cannot be said that the element of luck
entered into the affair at all, except, perhaps,
in so far as it enabled me to deliver my fly so
many times without mistake. I have, however,
taken many other and larger fish in practically
the same manner and by the employment of the
same tactics, and know the method to be sound
in theory and practice. For the solace of the
beginner who may attempt to practise the
method, let me add that in the beginning the
fish I took were, probably, a very small number
of those from which all thoughts of feeding were
driven by my bungling.

If a trout lying in a small pool and in plain
view, as was the one whose story has just been
told, could be induced to come up through six
feet of water to take the fly, is it not fair to
assume that an unseen fish may also be forced
to rise by the same tactics? Of course, in the
case of an unseen fish, the angler labours under
some disadvantage, because he is casting some-

what in the dark. In addition to ability to deliver many casts perfectly to a selected spot, he must also have the experience and knowledge that enable him to decide, at least approximately, where the fish may lie under the prevailing conditions. If his judgment in this particular is at fault his chances of rising the fish are gone. He should, therefore, assume that it occupies any of three or four positions, and for his first cast should choose that one of them which may be cast over with the least danger of disturbing the fish should it occupy any one of the others. If a rise be not had after a certain number of casts over the chosen position, the others should each be fished in turn.

The chance of putting down a fish for good will increase in proportion to the number of casts over each position, multiplied by the number of positions. That a rise is not had from the position first chosen will not prove that a fish does not occupy it, and the angler's subsequent casts will be made under increased difficulty, because of his efforts to refrain from further disturbing that water.

Before leaving this subject, and at the risk of becoming somewhat tedious and tiring my reader, I will relate the circumstances of the taking of an unseen fish by repeatedly casting over a chosen spot—in other words, of "forcing a rise." The incident has an added interest because a fellow angler witnessed it and was thereby convinced that a fish could be moved into position by the fly.

We were fishing the Brodhead, in Pennsylvania. It was in July and the day was very hot. The water was extremely low and very clear, and the upper reach of the stream just below the Canadensis bridge, which we had elected to fish, did not look big enough to hold a trout of any size. In one particular stretch there was a hundred yards of very shallow water, a small pocket on the right-hand bank being the only likely looking spot. I knew this stretch held many fine fish when the stream was in better condition, and I decided that this particular pocket might be the abiding-place of a good trout. As it was approaching the noon hour, I determined to go no farther up-stream but to spend a half hour experimenting on the little pocket.

The surface of the miniature pool was not over eight feet wide anywhere nor more than that in length, but its depth below a jutting rock which formed one side of it convinced me that it was worth trying, although there was no actual indication that a fish occupied it. The bottom was plainly discernible except in the swifter water near the head, and, as no fish could be seen, I selected the edge of this swift water upon which to place my fly. A dozen or more casts were made without any apparent effect, when suddenly a yellow gleam at the tail of the pocket, just after the fly had floated over the lip, disclosed a fine trout poised in the flattening water. Explaining the situation to my companion—who was now all excitement, having seen the fish, and who really did not believe it could be taken—on the spur of the moment I decided to try to prove my theory at the risk of losing the fish. I ceased casting to him. We watched him for probably two or three minutes, during which time he appeared to be keenly alert, when he quietly left his position and moved back up-stream into the swift water and out of sight. My opportunity had come, although my friend thought I had lost it. To make more certain that the colour of the fly played no part in the affair, I substituted a Silver Sedge for the Whirling Dun I had been using. After about a dozen casts with this fly there came the same yellow gleam,

and the fish was back into position again. This
time I continued casting, and, although he
seemed to "lean" toward the fly each time it
came down, he did not take it until it had
passed by ten times, finally rising deliberately
and fastening on the eleventh cast. He proved
to weigh one pound ten ounces.

To what conclusion does the observation of
this fish bring us? If he had been ready to feed
before the artificial appeared, is it likely that
he would have permitted it to pass over or
near him a score of times before taking? And
when he occupied what I call his feeding position, why did he allow the fly to pass ten times,
although exhibiting a certain interest in it each
time? It was never beyond his reach and could
easily have been taken. Was the desire to feed
being gradually aroused in him at each sight of
the fly? When he did take it, it was done with
such certainty that he must have believed it to
be a natural, although quite unlike anything he
had recently seen. One thing is certain, however. He was decoyed from one position to another on two occasions within a few minutes of
each other, and by a different pattern of fly
each time.

CHAPTER IV

WHERE AND WHEN TO FISH

THE swift streams in the eastern part of the
United States must, as a rule, be fished by
wading. Where it is possible, because of the
absence of trees and brush, to fish from the
bank, the angler's form is silhouetted sharply
against the background of sky, and, to overcome this disadvantage, he must retire some
distance from the edge of the bank, or, if he
wishes to come closer, must kneel or crouch to
avoid being seen by the fish. By casting from
the bank he will avoid the disturbance of the
water necessarily made by entering it, and this
is, of course, an advantage. On the other hand,
he is closer to the surface of the stream while
wading, in which position he is not so easily
seen, which is also an advantage. Offsetting the
latter, however, is the commotion made by his
movements, which, no matter how deliberate,
will make the trout nervous or apprehensive of
approaching danger. If he has shown himself,
even though the fish has been vigorously feed-

ing, he might just as well abandon any attempt to induce a rise, because the trout, having been warned by his careless approach, will have scurried away. The danger of putting down a fish in swift water is not so great because the ripples sent in advance of the angler make little headway and travel no great distance against a strong current.

To describe places where trout may be looked for under any and all circumstances, is practically impossible. Very often the fish will not be found where the angler thinks they should be. They are as full of notions and idiosyncrasies as anglers themselves, and one may hope to become familiar with their habitat in a general way only, and this after close study. I say "in a general way," because, while a big trout may be known to inhabit a certain pool, it does not follow that he is in the same spot to-day that he occupied yesterday or the day before. He may be looked for somewhere about, but a distance of even three or four feet from his previous known position may so place him as to prevent the angler from approaching without being seen. I am speaking of fish that are not rising. Of course, if they should be feeding upon the surface they are easily spotted.

Each pool or piece of water should be examined carefully after it has been fished. In this way the deeper holes, the nooks under the banks, and the crevices between boulders are discovered and marked down. If the angler is to spend much time on a stream that is new to him, it is even permissible to enter the deeper water quietly for the purpose of a thorough investigation; but under no circumstances should this be done if other anglers are upon the stream. As a rule, we are too careless of others' rights, and the ethics of fly fishing should be observed quite as closely as the code that governs our actions in any other sport.

A long, flat stretch of the stream is likely to contain many big fish, and must be approached in the most circumspect manner. The angler who hopes to take one of them should study the water carefully before entering it, and strive to determine just where the biggest fish lie. The character of the water and its temperature and the prevailing weather conditions are the data from which he must make his deductions.

By way of illustration, let us assume that the angler is upon the stream, prepared to fish it.

The day is one somewhere between the first

of May and the fifteenth of June. It is not too bright, and a light wind with a touch of summer in it is blowing up-stream. The water is running down after a light rain, and while not crystal clear is not much discoloured. It is about five-thirty o'clock of the afternoon, and the trout from below the stretch are coming on the feed. The flat to be fished is about one hundred and fifty feet long from where the water flows into it to where it rolls out again at the tail, and about fifty feet wide where the banks are farthest apart, narrowing, fan-like, to ten feet or less at the head. The current, gliding silently along the left bank (looking up-stream), shows the deep water to be on that side. These are ideal conditions, of course, and I have chosen them for that very reason. The angler is indeed fortunate who happens upon the stream when they prevail.

The natural place to look for trout under such conditions is anywhere along the left bank in the deep water. If flies are hatching—as in all probability they will be at this season—the angler need but watch for the rise that will indicate the position of the feeding fish. If these fish be small, as will be evidenced by the "staccato smack" made as the fly is taken, he

should move farther up-stream, because no
really big feeding fish need be looked for
where small ones are: *vice versa*, little fish rarely
feed in the same place and at the same time as
big ones. If no rise is seen, the task then is to
locate the fish, and, under the favourable conditions prevailing, it may be fairly assumed that
they are ready to feed. There will be one place
in the flat where more surface food collects than
in any other, and one place where more comes
down-stream because of converging currents.
In one of such places the biggest fish will be
found.

Wherever an eddy swirls gently against a
small cove in the bank, or the force of the current spends itself against a rock, making a dead
water or backwater above it, the fly may
search and find many fine trout. If the backwater at the head of the stretch is of an area
great enough to collect and hold the foam made
by the tumbling water, this is the spot from
which the angler may hope to secure one of the
best fish in the pool, if not *the* best. One of the
favourite feeding positions of a large trout is
under this foam, and the fly, placed carefully
again and again, often tempts him to move into
his feeding position when, at the beginning of

the casting, he lay outside of it. The fly should be dropped lightly on the foam and permitted to remain there until it is snatched away by the current.

It may happen that this particular part of the stretch does not contain one very large fish that "lords it" over a considerable area, but a number of fair-sized ones which, if feeding, will be somewhat scattered, and should be looked for in each of the places described.

Before or after the foam, backwater, and eddies have been tried, preferably before, the water on either side of the swiftest part of the current should be cast over, the fly being placed just at the bottom and at the side of the "lumpy" water. A fly cast to this position is extremely effective, dancing most naturally as it comes swiftly down-stream. This water should be tested thoroughly, the fly being placed always in the same spot and permitted to follow the same course for as long a distance as possible.

As daylight wanes, the fish often drop back to the tail of the stretch, sometimes feeding upon the very lip, or just above where the water begins to quicken before it spills out. This habit of trout may be due to their becoming less wary as dark approaches, and, consequently, quite willing to enter the shallower water, where they find it easier to pick up a few insects or a minnow or two than in the deeper, swifter water above. Wherefore, if the angler has been unsuccessful at the head of the stretch, let him, by travelling circuitously, find a position some distance below the lip, and fish the still water carefully as long as he can see his fly.

If the day is hot and bright, the water low and clear, and the fish not in any of the positions already described, they may be in either one of two places—along the bank or in the white water at the head.

If the fish are lying alongside of the bank they will prove to be as difficult to take as the most fastidious could wish. Knowledge of the crannies, depth, etc., will help the angler and make his task easier. But if the water is strange to him, and the trout must be searched for, his task is more complicated and he must exercise the greatest care in approaching. In many cases the stretches are lined on both sides by alders, willows, and the like, that make it impossible to cast without entering the water and, by so doing, forming ripples which, advancing ahead of the fly, warn the trout that danger is afoot. Exercising patience, he may walk slowly and quietly into the water at the tail of the stretch and as closely as possible to the bank the fish are under. Having attained the desired position, he should remain there long enough to allow all commotion made by his entry to cease, during which time no motion of the rod should be made, because the sight of any moving object will send the now alert trout scurrying, while the ripples will make him uneasy for a short time only. The horizontal cast should be used if possible. The fly should be floated down about a foot from the bank, and it should not be retrieved until it has travelled more than half the distance between the angler and the spot where it alighted. Casting should be continued until a mistake has marred the attempt, when the angler should desist, to resume after a short time has elapsed if the error has not been a glaring one.

When satisfied that no trout are within the section covered by the fly, the angler should lengthen his line and fish the fly a few feet above—always permitting the fly to travel over the water already fished. He should continue this until the maximum line that can be handled neatly without moving from the original position is being cast. When the line becomes unwieldy (in this method and position it is courting failure to

attempt anything over thirty-five to forty feet,
even if one is expert) an advance may be made
a few yards up-stream as closely to the bank as
the depth of the water and free casting space
will permit. As it is quite possible—and likely,
too—that a trout has been under the fly all the
while, but was not interested in it, the angler's
advance will drive him ahead, and indications
of this should be sharply looked for.   The discovery of the fish will save much valuable time,
for in that case the immediate stretch may be
abandoned, because any fish above the one seen
will have certainly taken alarm at the actions of
his fellow and will have lost all desire to feed
for some time.

If no fish is disturbed, search the bank carefully along its length, always remembering to
have the fly float down a considerable distance before retrieving.   The chances are quite
even, if the approach has been made carefully
and quietly, that a good fish will be risen.
In such water only skill of the highest type
is rewarded. If it is not possible to follow
along the bank under which the trout are lying,
the cast may be made from the opposite side;
but in this case a longer line should be used.
If the water must be entered to reach the bank

from the opposite side—and this, unfortunately, is usually the case—the angler should not move or allow his rod to move for some time after he has taken his position.

Having reached the head of the stretch, the angler may go over the eddies, backwater, and swift, and, if he meets with no response, the white water. This, above all places, is the difficult water to fish with the dry fly, and many anglers believe it to be quite impossible. If the dry fly be fished as is the wet fly—that is, cast in the swirl and allowed to drift about and down—it will become thoroughly drenched. But if it is placed properly and with due calculation, it is as easily kept dry and floating as upon any other part of the stream. The explanation lies in the fact that the fly is not placed directly upon the white water at all, if it be properly placed, but is cast to either side of the swift water, always on the side nearest the angler first, who should pick out the smooth looking spots upon which to place the fly. The fish which the wet fly angler takes directly from the centre of the current are taken on the dry fly by being induced to move out of their position. A very short line is used, and the fly is floated but a foot or two, being dropped lightly again and again. I will admit that trout are not taken from the white water in this way by the dry fly as frequently as they are with the sunk fly, but when one *is* taken it is usually a good fish.

On either side of the brink of the miniature fall above the white water may be seen boulders, seemingly acting as gatemen, directing the running waters to pass between. The current gliding swiftly toward them, deflected to right and left, reminds one of a flock of sheep all trying to get through a gap in the fence at the same time, those caught against the edge of the opening making little headway; and so it is with that part of the current which spends most of its force against the boulders. If this water be examined it will be discovered that considerable dead or back water is formed under the surface just above the boulders. Such places are among the selected retreats of *Salmo fario*.

A fly floated down from a point two feet above and retrieved just as it is about to go over the fall may produce a very pretty picture for the angler. If the fly upon its first appearance has been seen by the trout, he is often induced to rush at it, and, missing, goes headlong over the fall, instinct telling him, perhaps, that he may

find it below. Not to disappoint him, the angler
drops it immediately at the edge of the white
water, where it usually meets with a vicious
reception. Should all not come off as planned,
the fly may be cast again above the boulder and
retrieved as before. The fish may be tempted
to dart out and seize it after a dozen or more
casts. If hooked, he will come over the fall to
be dealt with in the smoother water below, and
the angler will not have missed the picture,
after all.

Native trout rarely occupy such positions,
but they should never be overlooked in streams
known to contain brown or rainbow trout.

Sometimes a short stretch of smooth, swift
water will be found sweeping silently along the
mossy bank just above the sentinel boulders at
the head of the white water. The bank is
probably shaded by overhanging rhododendron,
or alder growth, that lends to the water a peculiar, greenish hue. This stretch may be occupied by fine fish that, because of some effect
of light or shade, seem better able to detect the
approach of an angler or the connection of the
leader with the fly than do fish in similar waters
unshaded. A longer line is necessary here, and
great care should be exercised to refrain, as far

as possible, from entering that arc of a circle which is presumed to limit the range of the trout's vision. Difficulty will also be experienced in handling the line, owing to the greater length used and the rapidity with which it will be returned by the current. The danger of scaring the fish is minimised if the fly be delivered from a point almost directly in line with the current and the horizontal cast used. While not always necessary, the horizontal cast is better at all times, as the fly seems to cock more readily when thrown from this angle.

As a stretch of this character is usually of uniform depth along the greater part of its length, the fish may be in any part of it on a "feeding" day—a day when those below seemed to have been willing to feed. The fly should be placed at the foot of the stretch and on the side nearest the rod, and gradually worked, in the subsequent casts, toward the centre and head. This must be done slowly, however, and the fly should not be retrieved until it has come down some distance and has passed the spot where the first cast was delivered. The fish, in all probability, will be found near the middle of the stretch and to the side of the centre of the current nearer the bank. No attempt should be made to get closer, because the chance of having the fish come to the fly is greater than that of his taking, after the line has been seen.

When the prevailing conditions indicate that the trout are not in the open—in other words, are not fully engaged in feeding or in looking for food—they will usually be found lying near the bank. In such cases, the first attempt should be made at the tail or down-stream end of the swift, the fly being gradually worked up-stream a foot or so at a time and about a foot from the bank. It should be allowed to drift down to the foot of the stretch each time, and the casting continued until the entire length of the bank has been thoroughly searched. If the bank should be of gravelly or earthy formation it may be an overhanging one, having been undermined by the action of the current. The angler may be certain that this is so if that part above water shows a mass or network of bared roots. In this case the same procedure is followed, with the exception that the fly should be placed two feet, or even more, from the edge of the tangle, so that it may come the better within the angle of the fish's vision. It is quite obvious that a fly placed too close to the bank will be unseen by a fish occupying the hollow under it.

Great perseverance, even persistence, is required
to induce a fish to leave a retreat of this sort in
which he is snugly ensconced, but the attempt
should not be abandoned while it is certain
that no blunder has been made. Large trout
love these places, and coaxing one out is worth a
great deal of effort.

Long before a rise is effected, warning of the
possibility of its coming off is given by the
flash of a trout as he leaves his position under
the bank to assume another under the lane or
hatch of frauds. The trout is often a better
judge of distance than the angler, and when
this action of the fish is observed, any attempt
to make it easier for him by placing the fly
closer to the bank will, in all probability, put
a stop to further interest on his part. Difficult as it is to disobey the impulse to place the
fly where the fish was seen, it must be resisted,
because, while there is a possibility that the fish
may be risen, there is a greater likelihood that he
will be put down. For this reason the original
plan should be followed without deviation.
Ask him to come to the fly, and, while he may
seem diffident at first, he will finally accept the
invitation.

These swifts, or runs, as they are termed,

vary in length from fifteen to fifty feet, or more,
and the greater their length the more difficult
they are for the angler to cover without showing
himself. They are the narrows of the stream,
and, where the water is found to be of unvary-
ing depth, the fish may be looked for in any part
of them. The steady, rapid flow of the current
is admirably adapted to the use of the floating
fly, and is particularly attractive to those impatient ones who are unwilling to wait and
watch the fly's slow progress on the quieter
waters. Where the run being fished is distinctly "lumpy"—that is, where its speed is
greater because of the sharper incline in the
stream bed, and miniature waves are formed
that hurry down one after another—the floating
fly will be more difficult to handle, but is very
effective if well placed.

It was once my good fortune to see a stretch
of this character on the Neversink fished by a
friend, Mr. Walter McGuckin, who has been my
companion on many fishing excursions. He is
one of the best hands with a rod that I have
ever seen. His precision with the fly is remarkable, and I doubt if the grace and ease with
which he handles his line can be excelled. His
skill is fortified with a knowledge of trout gained

by over thirty-five years' experience on the waters of New York State. And, by the by, although he has used the wet fly for the greater portion of this time, he will now take his fish on the dry fly or not at all.

The weather of four seasons had been crowded into a single day—and this at the end of May. Although no insects of any kind had been seen, we had been able to mark a fish down the day before, when he had shown himself for an instant. Having fished the smooth water on either side of the centre of the current without engaging the fish's attention, my friend decided to "ride his fly" on top of the waves in the very swiftest part of the current. To do this effectively, and without having too much of the leader on the water, the chance of exposing himself to the fish was taken, as the fly had to be delivered from almost a right angle. However, it all came off correctly, and the fly, seeming barely to touch the water as it danced along, appeared even more lifelike than a natural insect. So, too, it must have appeared to the trout, for, after a number of casts had been made, a fish leaped directly from one wave to the one above, upon which was the fly, took it with mouth wide open and dived under. He was led gently to the still water below, and, although he proved to be a fine brown trout, his manner of taking the fly appealed to us more than his quality, and he was returned to the stream. The rise is the thing, and a dashing one of this sort makes the blood quicken as the dull *chug* of a fish taking under water never can.

When a trout is taken on a floating fly from beneath the tangled rubbish which collects about the submerged roots of a fallen tree or stump, the angler may attribute his success to common sense and reason more than to his dexterity in placing the fly. If we assume that the fish is under the tangle, taking advantage of the shade and protection it affords, is it logical to expect him to worm his way up through it to take a fly? And, as his head is invariably pointed up-stream, is it at all likely that a fly placed behind him will be observed? The answer is obviously, no! When a trout occupies a position of this character, it is always because of its proximity to water which will permit him the greatest freedom in securing food or in escaping from danger. He is often unwilling, and frequently unable, to dart rapidly down-stream when moved by either of these considerations, and the fly should be so presented that it will ask nothing uncommon of him.

Many anglers fail to take fish from these justly famed and wisely chosen domiciles of big trout, because of their reluctance or inability to estimate the odds on or against the sporting proposition. They are not ready to risk a ten cent fly for the purpose of properly fishing a spot which has cost them a hundred times as much to reach. With a few desultory casts—placed, usually, where they will do the least good and where, perhaps, a dozen others have been placed before that same day, sometimes within the hour—they move on. Congratulating themselves that they are safely out of a tight place, or comforting themselves with the thought that if a trout had been hooked it would have been lost anyway in the tangled mass, they abandon the spot—but always, I opine, with a lingering look backward. That these promising but difficult waters are prone to lure the angler into danger of hanging up solidly should make them the more interesting. When a good trout is taken from them, it is usually by a master of the craft, and no compassion need be wasted upon the fish—it has fallen into good and deserving hands.

The common practice of careless anglers is to

place the fly as close to the root or snag as they can, where there is but slight chance of its being seen by the fish—at least while it is upon the surface. Naturally, if the fly be sunk to a depth which will bring it within the horizontal plane of the fish's vision, it will be seen by him more readily. But, in fishing the floating fly, due allowance must be made for that portion of an imaginary circle enclosing the base of an inverted cone which will not come within view of the fish at the apex. This part will be directly over him, extending at an angle measured by the diameter of the root or snag under which he is hiding, this snag and the bank naturally being included in the calculation. To reach a fish in this position, or rather to place the fly so that it will be seen by him, an imaginary semicircle should be drawn about the spot, with a diameter equal to at least twice the known diameter of the obstacle, and the fly fished on this curved line until the circumference has been covered. Unless the angler can determine accurately the depth of the water or the submerged portion of the log, root, or whatever the obstacle may be, any allowance made over and above what appears necessary from the calculation will be to his advantage.

The down-stream part of the imaginary semi-circle will prove to be the least productive, for the reason that it is difficult to interest a fish from behind, he being more concerned about happenings in front of him. Nevertheless, considerable effort should be expended upon this part of it, as there is always a possibility of the fish being nearer the angler than has been calculated. Having fished it thoroughly, the water along the upper half of it may then be covered. The edge of this segment of the semicircle should be reached from a point nearly at right angles to its tangent, the angler retiring and assuming a position at a reasonable distance from the point being assailed. The rise may be looked for in that water where the swiftest part of the current flows directly toward and against the obstruction. And, as it is advantageous to have the fly cover a great distance upon the surface, it should be dropped a foot or two farther up-stream from the snag than when casting to the side of it. If the flow against the obstruction be studied there will be discovered on the edge of the current nearest the angler a spot whence the fly, being placed correctly, will be carried down to the obstacle and around it and will thus be exposed to the view of the trout without danger of drag or of "hanging up." The fly alone must travel in this part of the current, and the longer it travels in sight of the fish the greater is the likelihood of interesting him. Barring, always, the chance of error, the probability of taking the fish increases with each cast made. The situation confronting the angler who fastens to a fish in this water is a very trying one, and, if a fish so hooked is to be saved for the creel, tender methods will not avail. He must be unceremoniously bundled out and away from the dangerous spot, with every turn and crook of which he is familiar.

Aside from the fact that fishing well out from an obstacle gives a fish beneath it a more certain chance of seeing the angler's fly, the method has an additional advantage in that it lessens the risk of "hanging up" on one of the early casts—an accident that is very apt to cut short the angler's attempt if he tries to deliver his fly in places that are difficult to reach. But the angler who is unwilling to chance the loss of a fly by placing it close to a mass of drift or overhanging branches is not over-anxious to take sizable fish, and his success is usually meagre in proportion to the risk assumed.

Fishing the "edge of the circle" will frequently be found to be more effective than the accepted practice of searching the intricate tangles and openings, and is advocated as supplemental thereto.

A rift, properly speaking, is a shallow part of the stream where the current is quite rapid and more or less broken, and may be from ten yards in length to a mile or more. Where such water is spread from bank to bank and is very shallow, with but slight change in depth, little sport may be looked for. Random casts may bring a fish or two, but it is difficult to determine closely the positions in which trout may be; and, even if it were always possible to determine their position, the size of the fish would not induce the angler to waste much effort upon them. A strong rift of fair depth, however, probably harbours as many trout and will prove as productive to the average angler as any half dozen selected pools.

The character of these rifts changes so frequently that it would be useless to attempt to describe where trout may be found in them when the water is high. Furthermore, a cast here and there is quite as likely to fall within sight of roving fish that are not averse to travelling some distance to take the fly as a cast placed with intent to cover a particular spot. The most likely place, however, is along the side of the centre of the heaviest current, the fly being so placed that it will travel at the same speed as the leader and line, or a trifle faster.

When the stream begins to fall, instinct warns the trout that he must take up less unstable quarters. He fixes upon a permanent home, and only moves therefrom when there is another rise in the stream or during his nocturnal roamings in search of food.

In early spring, when the stream is high, trout are roaming about and may be found almost anywhere. When such conditions prevail it is not uncommon to hear anglers say that most of their fish were taken on the rifts. There are times during this season when it is more than likely that the rifts will be the only stretches that prove fruitful. When such is the case the angler, while he should never overlook the pools, should spend most of his time on the swift water.

On one occasion, while fishing a stream which empties into the Delaware, near Narrowsburg, N. Y., I walked two miles down-stream to the stretch which I had chosen for my afternoon's sport. My first cast was made close to two o'clock, and at six o'clock I had taken over twenty fish, four of which, weighing over five and one half pounds, I killed, and twice as many more of the same size I returned to the stream. I got out of the stream about at the same spot I had entered it, having fished not over one hundred yards in four hours. The fish were taken in a broken rift; it seemed as if each rock in it was the hiding-place of a good one; and, though the current was quite swift, the floating fly was taken in each case slowly and deliberately. They were, it is true, not so large as one might have hoped to get in some of the deeper pools, but fair fish, nevertheless; and, as about half of them were rainbow trout, interest in the sport did not flag for a moment.

In a short rift or run forming the connecting-link between two pools, fish from both will be found occupying it when feeding, occasionally during the day, but usually at night, at which time minnows and other small fish may be picked up. Sometimes a good fish will remain in this water, but, because of the facility afforded him for entering it from above or below, this is not often the case. While this stretch is less fruitful than another which I will try to describe, it should never be carelessly fished; and, if the instructions given in this chapter for fishing the swift are followed, the effort should not go unrewarded. Many of these short rifts are met with in a day's fishing and too often are slighted by those careless anglers who seem anxious only to have their flies upon the surface of pools. They should be given careful attention, let conditions be what they may.

There are other rifts where the current seems to be travelling at its greatest speed and where the fall is sharp and continuous. Where the decline ends abruptly a pool is formed; where it is gradual, and the force of the current is spent, it spreads, fan-like, over the formation of gravel and stones, finally flowing to one bank or the other, forming another pool or another rift. The fish occupying these longer rifts or rapids may not be the largest in the stream, but are likely to be well above the average in size and worth trying for. Along both sides of the swiftest part of the current the fly may be floated successfully. A long line is inadvisable unless the angler has mastered the difficulty of handling it under such circumstances, because it is returned very quickly. He should pick out the "oily" looking spots upon which to place the fly, because there is less likelihood of its being drenched than if it is placed in the breaking water.

Conforming to the custom among many anglers, and for lack of a better term, I include in the term "rifts" those parts of the stream which, in my opinion, are the finest of all places to fish. I refer to the stretches where great boulders, and small ones too, protruding above the surface of the water, divide the current, which flows quietly but steadily between and around them.

In many cases it will be found that the banks on either side of such stretches, while not precipitous, are higher than where they border the wider parts of the stream. The bed being narrower, the depth of water will be found greater. For these reasons such sections are chosen by trout when the stream is low. The shady part of this water, if there be any, should be approached first, particularly if the weather be bright and the water low. Each boulder, in turn, should be carefully and thoroughly searched with the fly. The first attempt may be made between any two rocks, not too widely separated, at the bottom or down-stream end of the stretch, the fly being placed directly between and a foot above them. After several casts have been made the fly may be thrown a foot or two farther up-stream but in line with the previous casts.

Fishing the fly between such boulders serves a double purpose. As the fish lie alongside or just above them, the fly is readily seen from either position, and if it is taken near one of them the angler is saved the necessity of fishing the others, the indications being that the fish are ready to feed and that they may be lured away from their stands. On most occasions, however, the fish will be found just above the boulder and on the shady side, and the fly, persistently delivered in that position, will attract many of them.

The angler should remember that the back-water formed by the current flowing against the up-stream side of a boulder is a favourite haunt of brown trout, and should assume that the fish in the stretch occupy such positions until some indication is given that they do not. He should so present the fly that the fish is afforded a fair view of it and is not asked to come too far to take it. Rough water should be avoided when possible; but the fly should be floated on or near

the swiftest part of the current, and this will usually be found close to the boulder.

When the boulders in a stretch are irregularly
scattered, the course of the current being deflected by them so that the water twists and
turns to escape the obstacles in its path, each
one may harbour a good fish.   Not one of them
should escape the attention of the angler.   Even
those which appear to be in shallow water are
worthy of consideration and sometimes yield
large fish.   The eddies behind them may be
fished as much as he pleases, but he should not
forget that on the up-stream side the greater
number of fish will be found.   He should avoid
haste, and also the conclusion that because a
fish is not risen in one spot there is none occupying it.   If, by carelessness, he drives out a
fish, his chance of taking one higher up in the
same stretch is jeopardised.

Where the current is direct in its flow, travelling, apparently, through what might be called
a lane of boulders, the fish, if feeding, may be
looked for in its middle along its entire course,
as well as beside and above the rocks.   Beginning at the bottom, the water for a very
short distance may be covered from a point
directly below; but after that the casts should

be made at an angle of about forty-five degrees
from either side, so that the fish, which may have
been under the fly and have been unmoved by
it, will not see the angler or his line.   A sight of
the line moves fish in a way that is very distress-
ing to the angler responsible for it.

Of similar character are those stretches where
the rapid current dashes against and around
the boulders in them.   From a distance one of
these stretches appears to be a mass of tossing
water, where the dry fly might be expected to
be hopelessly out of place.   In such parts of
the stream the fall is quite sharp, the water
tumbling over a succession of diminutive falls,
presenting, when viewed from below, an appearance of great turbulence.   Upon close inspection, however, there will be found between
the boulders miniature pools, popularly called
"pockets," where the current, while strong, is
not direct, a great part of its force being spent
in seeking new channels.

Beginning at the bottom row of the pockets,
the tail of the lowest is cast over with as short
a line as may be used consistently with precision.   Where the water glides swiftly over the
lip of the pocket the fly should be placed above
and in such position that in its course down-

stream it will pass close to the boulder which is deflecting the deeper and stronger part of the current. As the fly passes the boulder it should be lifted quickly but quietly from the water. A false cast or two should be made to dry it, and then it should be placed in exactly the same position as before, this procedure being continued until a rise is effected or the angler is prompted to abandon the spot. The fly may then be advanced a short distance at a time, the longitudinal position remaining the same, until the water in a straight line up-stream between the boulder and the head of the pocket is covered. The other side should then be fished in the same manner, and this without the angler having changed his own position, which should have been assumed at the start with reference to the availability of all parts of the water.

Each pocket will present practically the same features. The depth may be greater in one, the current stronger in another, but the boulders at the head and tail should be the objective points for the angler's fly in every case. Where the depth is great or the current strong, more persistence upon the part of the angler is demanded—compensated, as a rule, by a larger fish. Where the water, with but a gentle wrin-

kle, slips by the boulder and does not break
into a fall, the fly should be placed a yard above
and directly in front of the boulder, and should
not be retrieved until it has passed some distance
down-stream. A fish in the dead water may
often be tempted to come down after the fly, and
when this happens the whole scene is enacted in
plain view. There is nothing quite so exciting
as this in the whole sport of angling except, perhaps, casting to and inducing a fish to rise that
is lying in plain view.

Trout frequently take up stations in the backwater or eddy which is formed under and behind
the miniature falls in these rapid stretches.
When in this position they are inaccessible to
the dry fly angler. They belong entirely to the
wet fly man who is familiar enough with the
habits of the fish to drop his fly above the brink
of the fall, allowing it to be carried over and
then under the water, so that, if it is caught in
the backwater, it is presented directly to the
fish, which rarely refuses to take one that comes
so easily. When evening comes on, however,
the dry fly angler has his opportunity. The
sizable fish which select these retreats during
the bright days drop down-stream as darkness
approaches, and, if not cruising, will be found

just where the current spends itself, or under and below the little eddies to the side. These eddies should be scrutinised closely if insects are upon the water. The presence of the fish will be indicated by the rise to the flies which collect there. Should there be no insects about, the fish may be induced to rise by casting repeatedly in the quieting water.

Perhaps no water on our American streams appeals more to the average angler than a beautiful pool; and yet rarely does this water fulfil the promise it seems to hold out. That pools do contain trout, and sometimes very large ones, is true; but the fact that the fish may remain unmoved, after every artifice of the angler has been exhausted in an attempt to induce them to rise, is very discouraging. This not unusual experience may be the foundation for the belief many anglers have that the larger fish have ceased to be surface feeders and cannot be persuaded to rise to a small insect. To get one of these big fish with the floating fly the angler must have "luck"—that luck which brings him upon the stream when the fish are near the surface. Success on waters of this kind depends quite as much upon the mood of the fish as upon the skill of the angler.

If the fish are feeding, or are ready to feed, upon winged insects, they will be found in a position from which the angler's fly may be seen, in which event he may hope to bring them to the artificial. But no amount of skill will induce a rise if the fish are hidden in the strongholds with which these rocky pools abound. It is absurd to expect that a big fish, lying near the bottom of a pool which may have six or eight feet of water in it, will come that distance upon the first appearance of a tiny morsel of food upon the surface. A fish that has retired to deep water is not interested in food; or, if he is, only caddis larvæ, dobsons, etc., that may be picked up on the bottom, or some other sort of food considerably under the surface, will attract his attention.

Trout fortunate enough to escape the many dangers which beset them in our streams grow to great size and become largely nocturnal feeders. Night feeding is an instinct of the fish, though the smaller ones are forced by the appetite of youth to seek food in daylight, also. This is why a pool that looks as if it should contain a big fish (and probably does) yields but a few dandiprats when the condition of the water has been unchanged for any length of

time. The big fish are not ravenous enough
to be seeking food all of the time, and the little
chaps have undisputed possession of the open
water. A wonderful change in the mood of
these large fish takes place when the stream
is freshened after a fall of rain. The artificial
fly is then taken in the most deliberate and certain manner—taken by the fish as if they knew
it as a member of a family with which they have
been acquainted all their lives, although it may
not bear the slightest resemblance to any living
insect. At such times the angler is apt to lose
faith in the much-vaunted wariness and cunning
of the fish and may foolishly ascribe his remarkable success to his own skill. Whether the
change of water invigorates trout, or instinct
tells them that they may expect food to be
washed down to them, it is certain that the desire to feed is aroused, and they are at these
times neither fastidious nor discriminating.

Several years ago on a stream in Sullivan
County, the name of which I have promised to
forget, I was in the brook just after the top of a
flood and found the fish so willing that, for the
particular day, at any rate, I was ready to believe
the story told of some northern waters where
the fish "were so numerous and so hungry that

one had to hide behind a tree to bait the hook."
Nearly every cast brought a slow, deliberate,
businesslike rise—all large fish for so small a
stream. I killed two fish that weighed one
pound five ounces, and one pound nine ounces,
respectively. One of these fish had two crawfish
in its stomach, freshly taken; the other had a
small stone catfish, pretty well digested; there
was nothing else in either—not an insect of any
sort. The next day was practically a repetition
of the previous one—two fish killed, both just
over one pound five ounces. The stomach and
gullet of one were absolutely empty; the other
contained a single June-bug, freshly taken, and,
among a number of other insects, a water-
strider, long thought by anglers to form no part
of the trout's menu. I have never been able
to quite satisfy myself that this particular experience was of any great value except that it
strengthened my belief that trout are moved to
feed by changes in the stream caused by flood
waters running down. Perhaps, also, it tended
to prove that there were more big fish in the
stream than I would have believed without the
experience. All my fish were taken at the lips
of the pools which abound in this rock-bedded
stream, and I devoted my time exclusively to

those places, in the hope of securing a really good fish. No small fish rose to the fly, although they are a-plenty in the stream. They had evidently been driven to other water by fear of their older brothers.

The greatest essential to success in fly fishing, wet or dry, is stream knowledge; by which I mean, not necessarily familiarity with the stream actually being fished, but that general knowledge, based on careful study of the habits of the fish, that enables the angler to select the proper part of the current in which to place the fly. Such selection is of the greatest importance when pools are being fished—it is next in importance to keeping out of sight of the trout. Under no circumstances should a pool be approached with the idea of placing the first cast in what appears to be the likeliest spot, as there is always danger of frightening the fish off if he should happen to be somewhere else in the pool. Before a fly is placed on the water, a careful study should be made of its depths and currents. If the large fish are surface feeding, they may be looked for in two places particularly: at the very lip of the pool or in the eddies at the head.

The indication that a fish is feeding at the lip

or bottom of a pool is unmistakable. While the
actual taking of the insect may be accomplished
quietly, the fish lies sometimes so close to the
surface where the water spills out that the
sharp recovery necessary in the quickening
water reveals his position. This is a difficult
fish to take, for the reason that, lying as he
does in the shallower water—which, as a rule,
has a smooth surface—he is very apt to see the
angler. A long line must be used, which adds
to the difficulty, as it is almost impossible to
keep the line out of the swift water below the
lip which snatches the fly away from the fish
before he has even had a good look at it. A
proper presentation may be made, however, and
this annoying drag avoided, if the cast is so delivered that the line falls upon one of the stones
or boulders which form the lip of the pool. The
fly will then float naturally, without being pulled,
until it reaches the point where the water spills
out, which point it must be allowed to pass
before being retrieved. If no rise is effected
the cast may be repeated, and continued as long
as the fish is still in position. No connection
need be looked for, however, unless the fly is
placed fairly close to and above the fish, and
marked acceleration of pace avoided. Where

there are no kindly boulders to help the angler in his deception, a chance—though a remote one—may be taken by presenting the fly in the hope that it may be taken at once, because of its accurate delivery, and before there is any drag upon it.

If, at the moment of the angler's arrival at a pool, there are no insects upon the water there will be no rise to indicate the position of a fish. But it does not follow that one is not in position and ready to feed. In this case even greater care should be exercised in approaching the lip of the pool than if a rise had been actually observed.. If the angler does his work well, and has a sharp eye, the fish may often be seen lying along the side of the current as the water spills out, or just above some small boulder or other obstruction to the water's course. Sometimes the boulders may be completely under water, but their presence is denoted by a wrinkling of the surface, and the fish may be looked for just above them.

The angler must work out the problem of properly presenting the fly at each pool. In no case, however, where the fish is seen or his position is indicated by his activities should the fly be cast directly over him. It should always be cast to one side or the other, slightly above, and at an angle. This suggestion may be safely followed in every case where fish are seen and it is possible to so cast from the position occupied by the angler. When the fish are found to be occupying positions at the tail of pools—whether it be early morning, or just at dusk, or, as it sometimes happens, at midday— they are almost invariably ready to feed; and, while not always interested in insects, they are frequently induced to take the artificial because it appears close to them. Though there may have been no indication that the large fish have dropped back from the deeper water to the lip of the pool, the angler's actions should always be governed by the assumption that they are in that position until he is convinced that they are not. If he has been incautious the widening wake marking the fish's swift dart up-stream makes it quite certain that the hope of taking a trout from that particular pool must be deferred. Small fish occupying this "tail position" are as easily frightened off by sight of the angler as the large ones are, and their alarm, being communicated to the fish above, destroys whatever chance there might otherwise have been on the upper water. It is the carelessness with which the average angler over-looks this important part of the pool that is re-sponsible for the many failures registered on what should be productive water.

It frequently happens, particularly when the water is low and bright and has not been re-cently disturbed, that trout are lying a few yards above the lip of the pool in the quiet water. The presence of the fish is disclosed by the wake made by him in his rush for a fly that has been presented somewhere near him. The direction the fish is taking is easily discernible, and, if he is headed down-stream—which is often the case—the situation is one that requires the gentlest possible handling. The angler should remain motionless, leaving his fly upon the water even at the risk of having the line become entangled about his feet, because the fish, being headed in the angler's direction, will be quick to detect any motion; and the rod should not be moved under any consideration. The fish, after having composed himself, will be headed up-stream again and, if not actually seen by the angler, may be assumed to be where the wake ended.

It is quite usual for a fish, after having made a rush toward the fly, to abandon the chase

when the fly approaches too closely to the spill,
to assume a position where he stopped, and to
wait there for another insect to come down.
This is the angler's opportunity; but if it is
to be of any advantage to him deliberation
must mark his every action. The fly must
be dropped gently over the marked spot and
should not be retrieved until it has passed below the rod. It will be difficult to overcome
the impulse to retrieve the fly, even though it
is getting farther beyond control all the time;
but, as the fish has possibly been interested in
it and, having turned, will immediately detect
any action of the rod and be off at once, such
impulse must be resisted. By stripping the
line in with the disengaged hand, the fly may be
recovered and presented again. Until the fly is
taken by the fish, or until the angler is convinced that it will not be taken, every motion
should be very deliberate. If the fish is not
risen on the first cast, each succeeding throw
should be made a little farther up-stream than
the previous one, until the point where the fish
was first seen is reached. The fly should not be
retrieved in any case until it has passed over
the water covered before—and it should travel
in the same lane after each cast. A fish spotted

as described will surely fall to the rod if the
angler is careful, and his taking will afford some
of the most pleasurable moments spent upon the
stream.

When the angler decides to abandon the lower
end of the pool, it is much wiser for him to use
a longer line to reach the upper water than it
is to advance up-stream, because by wading up
he may frighten a fish lying in the part of the
pool already covered and thus warn off the
ones above. The entire pool should be carefully scanned for indications of feeding fish
before any attempt is made to cast over the
upper part of it. The eddies on either side of
the main current at the head of the pool should
be given particular attention. Should a large
fish inhabit the pool the eddy will be his
dining-room. He will occupy it, however, only
at certain intervals, and, if the angler should
be fortunate enough to arrive at a time when
he is seeking food, it ought to yield a fine
trout. Rarely meeting competition because of
their size, the fish in these eddies are very deliberate in their feeding—securing such insects
as may be on the surface with but little effort.
For this reason many opportunities are missed
by the unobservant angler who fails to notice

the gentle wrinkling of the surface, or the small
bubble left upon it, as the fish sucks in some
tiny insect, and by the careless angler who sees
the slight disturbance, and attributes it to a
small fish. Some of the largest fish I have ever
killed gave no indication of their size as the fly
was taken, and not until they had fastened did I
realise how heavy they were. The slightest indication of action in the eddy should be investigated thoroughly with the fly; for, while only
a small fish may be taken in one, the next may
produce "the big fish."

Throwing to a fish in the eddy of a pool requires some care, but a close study of the currents will make it comparatively easy. Trout
always lie with heads to the current, and those
in an eddy are no exception; consequently, they
will be headed *down-stream*, or against the current, which is flowing *up*. This position of the
fish must be taken into consideration when the
fly is to be presented from below, and the
angler will find that his greatest difficulty will
be in keeping out of sight. How he may do
this he must decide for himself, but, even at
the risk of being seen, he should cast up-stream
from *directly below* the fish; *i. e.*, from a position
on the same side of the swift current as the eddy

he is fishing. If the fly is dropped in that part of the current which is turning up-stream it will be carried to the fish in a natural manner, and if care has been taken in placing the line loosely in the comparatively dead water below, the progress of the fly will not be impeded. If the fish has been well spotted, the fly should be dropped a foot or two below him, and always in that current which will bring it directly to him. In this particular situation the first cast should be the telling one, because if the fly is not taken it is not returned to the angler immediately, and its retrieve against the current is likely to be disturbing to the fish. If the fly has been carried over and beyond the spot where the rise was seen, it does not follow that it has passed over the fish and been refused. He may be backing up under it, and may take it a yard from where he is presumed to be, if it travel that far. However, if satisfied that the fly is not going to appeal to the fish—which conclusion should not be reached until the fly is no longer in a natural position—the retrieve may be made very slowly and carefully, after which the angler may wait a minute or two, or until the fish rises again.

Sometimes the fly will be carried by the eddy

toward the swift, down-stream current and be
caught in it. In this event, it is easily retrieved
without disturbing the water in the vicinity of
the fish, and may be presented again immediately.
A fish should not be given up while continuing
to rise steadily; he will become accustomed to the
artificial, and will take it in time, if its action is
not unnatural. An eddy should be fished in the
same careful manner whether a fish is seen feeding in it or not; but, in the latter case, while a
fish may be in position and ready to feed, the
varying currents and the difficulty encountered
in attempting to retrieve the fly delicately
against them destroy its natural action, and
prevent, to a certain extent, proper simulation
of a "hatch." The fly can cover but a short
distance before it is necessary to retrieve it, and
this makes for rather tedious work, because it
must be brought back slowly and gently until
it is out of the eddy before it is taken from the
water. In this connection, it may be borne in
mind that it is possible to decoy a fish from the
eddy by placing the fly on the edge of the swift,
down-stream current nearest the eddy, permitting it to float down three or four yards each
time. If a half dozen casts have brought no response, it is better to discontinue casting than

to risk driving the fish to another part of the pool, and thus disturb some other fish that might have fallen to the rod later had it remained unmolested.

CHAPTER V

THE IMITATION OF THE NATURAL INSECT

WITHIN a very recent period, it has been asserted, upon scientific authority, that fish are colour-blind. If this be true, though it is difficult for the mere angler to understand how it may be proven, the theory of those who believe that it is necessary to imitate in the artificial fly the colour of the insects upon which trout feed must be abandoned.

Writing upon the subject no longer ago than 1904, Sir Herbert Maxwell, certainly a competent observer, said: "My own experience goes to convince me that salmon, and even highly educated chalk-stream trout, are singularly indifferent to the colours of flies offered to them, taking a scarlet or blue fly as readily as one closely assimilated to the natural insect. Probably the position of the floating lure, between the fish's eye and the light, interferes with any nice discrimination of hue from reflected rays."

Cotton and the many angling writers who followed him all dwelt with insistence upon the necessity for close imitation, especially in relation to colour. In 1740 John Williamson stated the principle in the following words: ". . . . as the great Difficulty is to obtain the Colour of the *Fly* which the Fish take at the Instant of your Angling, it is impossible to give any certain Directions on that Head; because several Rivers and Soils are haunted by peculiar Sorts of Flies, and the Flies that come usually in such a Month of the Year, may the succeeding Year come almost a Month sooner or later as the Season proves colder or hotter. Tho' some Fish change their Fly once or twice in one Day, yet usually they seek not for another Sort, till they have for some Days glutted themselves with a former, which is commonly when those Flies are near Death, or ready to go out." Then, giving some simple instructions in regard to tying flies, he quotes Walton: "But to see a Fly made by an Artist is the best Instruction; after which the Angler may walk by the River, and mark what Flies fall on the Water that Day, and catch one of them, if he see the *Trouts* leap at a Fly of that Kind. . . ." Williamson's book was practically a compilation, containing the best of what had been written by anglers before him, together with his own observations.

From Williamson's time no work on fly fishing seemed complete unless instructions were given in the art of fly making, with a description of the sorts and colours of furs, silks, feathers, etc., suitable for the imitation of the natural insects held to be so necessary; but until the appearance in 1836 of Ronalds's "Fly Fishers' Entomology," it cannot be said of any author that the instructions given by him were the result of scientific study. Ronalds was most thorough in his investigation, and his experiments in regard to the senses of taste and hearing of trout are extremely interesting and instructive. While his conclusions run counter to the opinions of many other angling writers, to my mind they appear logical and are convincing; and I think he proves that trout do not have the senses of taste and hearing developed to the degree of acuteness attributed to them by other writers. Following some advice as to the choice of flies, Ronalds says: "It should never be forgotten that, let the state of weather or the water be what it may, success in fly fishing very much depends upon showing the fish a good imitation, both in colour and size, of that insect which he has recently taken; an exact resemblance of the *shape* does not seem to be quite as essential a requisite as that of colour, since the former varies according to the position of the insect either in or upon the water; but a small fly is usually employed when the water is fine, because the fish is then better enabled to detect an imitation and because the small fly is more easily imitated. The resemblance of each particular colour, etc., is not required to be so exact as in the case of a large fly." Notwithstanding his evident preference for colour over shape or form, Ronalds was careful to have the proportions of his imitations exact. The many editions of his work that have been issued, and the frequent reference made to him by later writers, is evidence that his opinions are held in high regard by anglers.

About three years before the "Fly Fishers' Entomology" appeared, Professor James Rennie, in his "Alphabet of Scientific Angling," ridiculed the theory of imitation. He says: "It is still more common, however, for anglers to use artificial baits, made in imitation or pretended imitation, of those that are natural. I have used the phrase 'pretended imitation' as strictly applicable to by far the greater number of what are called by anglers artificial flies, because these rarely indeed bear the most distant resemblance to any living fly or insect whatever, though, if exact imitation were an object, there can be little doubt that it could be accomplished much more perfectly than is ever done in any of the numerous artificial flies made by the best artists in that line of work. The fish, indeed, appear to seize an artificial fly because, when drawn by the angler along the water, it has the appearance of being a living insect, whose species is quite unimportant, as all insects are equally welcome, though the larger they are, as in the case of grasshoppers, so much the better, because they then furnish a better mouthful. The aim of the angler, accordingly, ought to be to have his artificial fly calculated, by its form and colours, to attract the notice of the fish, in which case he has a much greater chance of success than by making the greatest efforts to imitate any particular species of fly." That this statement caused considerable discussion—probably because it was made by a professor of zoology—is evidenced by the appearance in 1838 of "A True Treatise of the Art of Fly-Fishing," written by those strong advocates of the imitation theory, William Shipley and Edward Fitzgibbon, who devoted a whole chapter to controverting the professor's theories, calling upon the writings of Bainbridge, Best, Taylor, Davy, Ronalds, and others in support of their opinions, concluding with the statement that "they flattered themselves that they had triumphantly done so." It seems to me that, though they argued with vigour and vehemence, they have proven nothing, conclusively, except their ability to place a construction upon the professor's statements that afforded them an opportunity for the discussion. A careful reading of Rennie shows that he merely expressed the opinion that the greatest efforts of the angler should be to make his fly one that would attract the notice of the fish by its form and colour, rather than to imitate any particular species of fly. To be sure, we have no knowledge of what his ideas with regard to form and colour were; we may assume, however, that he believed that if a red fly four inches long with yellow and blue wings and a green tail would attract the fish, such would be the fly to use. The illustration is absurd, of course; but we have a right to infer that his belief was that any form or colour which would attract the fish would do. He advanced the theory that the trout took the artificial because they were near-sighted; apparently he did not believe that they took it because they were colour-blind.

The English creation known as the "Alexandra," representing absolutely nothing in insect life (at least to eye of man), strongly supports Professor Rennie's theory. Its effect upon trout has been so deadly that it has been suggested by many English anglers that its use should be barred upon some streams. In the same class with the Alexandra might be placed our own American nondescript, the "Parmacheene Belle," the invention of Mr. Henry P. Wells, whose theory was, "An imitation of some favourite food is in itself sufficient under all circumstances, provided it is so conspicuous as readily to be seen . . . and the fly in question was made, imitating the colour of the belly fin of the trout itself." This theory may be sound enough, but in this particular application of it one is asked to believe that the trout is inordinately fond of the belly fin of its relatives, which seems to me to be straining credulity overfar. To some old cannibalistic fish these fins may be attractive. I do not deny it, for I do not know; but in my own experience I have not known them to be plucked or bitten from the victim; nor are they found floating about loosely. The Parmacheene Belle is undoubtedly an imitation of the belly fin of a trout, but it is not an imitation of any favourite food of the fish. Its value as a lure is well known to those who fish in the lakes and streams of Canada and Maine, but trout do not take it because they recognise it as a familiar article of diet. They probably take it because of its brilliant colour, in which respect it embodies Professor Rennie's idea of what a "fly" should be. Being made up of reds and whites, it probably reflects more light than do sombre-hued patterns and, consequently, is the more easily seen. As a rule, it is taken under water, and most often after it has sunk to considerable depth.

Speaking of the Alexandra, Mr. Halford says: "It certainly is not the imitation of any indigenous insect known to entomologists; possibly the bright silver body moving through the river gives some idea of the gleam of a minnow. Long ere this its use should have been prohibited on every stream frequented by the *bona-fide* fly-fisherman, as it is a dreadful scourge to any water, scratching and frightening an immense proportion of the trout which are tempted to follow it." If this means anything, it means that trout are at first attracted by the fly or lure, but upon closer inspection discover the cheat, and, taking it uncertainly, are often

slightly pricked, or, refusing it entirely, are
sometimes scraped by the hook as they turn
away. This criticism, it seems to me, might be
directed equally well against any creation of
feathers, fur, and tinsel that is fished sunk.

While rather off the main point, I may be so
bold as to say that, while the sunk fly method
does not appeal to me at all, I cannot readily see
that it scratches many fish or frightens them
in any way; and, if it did, the recollection of the
affair would not linger long enough in the trout's
memory to injure the chances of his being taken
the next day on a dry fly, or even on another
sunk one. Mr. G. E. M. Skues, who advocates
the use of the sunk fly on the same streams
where correct imitations are presented to rising
fish, says that he presents imitations of the
nymphæ in the positions occupied by the naturals; that he rarely scratches a fish, and hooks
but very few foul. The inference in this case
might be that the trout fastens to an imitation
more readily than to an Alexandra—one really
deluding the fish by its natural appearance, the
other exciting only its curiosity or ire.

While exhibiting an admirable filial loyalty,
many of us have been prone to be governed
by tradition, and the education we received in

the beginning from our fathers.   With few ex-
ceptions, we have trudged along the beaten
path, looking rarely to right or left, but backward a great deal, using the same flies our
fathers used before us, emulating their methods,
and admiring their successes.   We have overlooked the fact that we are contending with
conditions that have decreased the number of
native trout, and that would have taxed even
the great skill with which we have endowed
those of loving memory.   I remember that one
of my father's favourite flies was the Queen-of-
the-Waters.   Naturally it became one of mine,
and I used it religiously—remembering its successes, forgetting its failures.   A story connected
with this fly may prove interesting, and perhaps
tend to show how close I was to becoming a
confirmed colourist, or, rather, a strong believer
in the trout's ability to detect colour.

Many years ago, while preparing for a short
trip to the stream, I discovered that I did not
have a single Queen-of-the-Waters in my fly
book.   On my way to the railroad station I
stopped in a tackle shop and asked for a dozen
of that pattern.   The clerk was unable to find
any in stock, but suggested that I try a dozen
called King-of-the-Waters.   Although there was,

in fact, little similarity between these two patterns except in the name itself, this seemed
sufficient to my ignorant mind, and I took them.
The following day, upon the stream, my cast of
three flies (I was a wet fly angler then) was
never without a King-of-the-Waters—and not a
fish did I take with it. I attributed my non-
success to the pattern of fly, and it never oc-
curred to me at the time that very few fish were
taken at all that day, although many anglers
were on the stream. The next morning, when I
opened my fly book, I found that a great deal
of the red dye used upon the silk body of the
fly had come off on the drying pad. The body
of the fly was now a beautiful pink. Out of
curiosity I wet the fly, and the pink body
turned a brilliant red. I thought the thing
over, and decided that I had stumbled upon an
explanation of the failure of the fly to take the
day before. The body of the fly originally was
red and was evidently meant to appear so to
the trout. When wet, however, it had turned a
muddy brown. With most of the colour washed
out, the fly turned a darker shade when wet,
became really red, and stayed red. I determined that if this was the colour the trout
wanted, they should have it, and I soaked a half

dozen flies in a tumbler of water, pressing and squeezing every bit of dyestuff out of them that I could. They were all pink-bodied when I had finished with them. Recollections of the following day are still fresh in my mind. The fish seemed frantic to get my fly. I used one as the stretcher, and it was taken almost to the utter exclusion of the other patterns above. I remember that, while sitting upon a boulder in midstream tying another pink fly on in place of the hand dropper, as an experiment, I lost it in the swift current, and felt almost as badly as if I had lost a friend. The fly used as a dropper was taken readily, but not so often as when used as a stretcher, yet often enough to make me feel that I had made a great discovery. Since then, however, I have often wondered if it really were a discovery, or if, indeed, the old Queen-of-the-Waters, under the circumstances and conditions prevailing at the time, would not have been just as killing, and probably just as great a failure the preceding day.

Many years have passed, and I am still using the pink-bodied fly, modified in form, however, but never the Queen-of-the-Waters. I cannot say that I think it takes any better than the Whirling Dun or the Pale Evening Dun, which

are among my favourites. Frequently, when I
have found the pink-bodied fly taking well, I
have changed immediately to one of the others,
and have found no marked difference in their
taking qualities. The pink-bodied fly in its
present form—that is, tied in accordance with
my own practice—has upright wings and a tail,
and in appearance is not unlike the Red Spinner.
It has been dubbed the "Pink Lady" by one of
my friends, a name that it seems destined to
carry, as it has already appeared by that name
in a tackle dealer's catalogue. As to whether
or not the trout is attracted by the brilliancy
of the body, or by the rib of gold tinsel that
gives it a fillip other flies lack, or because it
bears a fairly close resemblance to the Red
Spinner, I cannot venture an opinion. That it
is a taking fly, however, I have demonstrated
many times upon the stream. I am inclined to
believe that its typical form, rather than its
colour, appeals to the fish. Opposed to my opinion, however, is that of many of my friends who
use it, one of whom, in particular, contending
that the pink-bodied fly will take fish anywhere at any time. He firmly believes that its
colour constitutes its charm. It is an interesting fact, considered in this connection, that the

gentleman himself is, to some extent, colour-blind.

Objects floating upon the surface of a shallow stream reflect the colour of the bottom in varying degree, according to their density. A number of white objects floating above a moss or grass covered bottom reflect different tones of green, that one which is most opaque showing the darkest shade, and each one reflecting a lighter tone in proportion to the amount of light that filters through it. It is true, of course, that a yellow insect floating over this same bottom would reflect a shade of green all its own, and it is but natural to assume that if the same shade or tint of yellow is used in the artificial, its employment would more nearly approximate the effect of reflection upon the natural insect; but if the exact shade or tint is important, the effect is not produced unless the same amount of light passes through both natural and artificial. The use of the hook itself precludes the possibility of any delicate imitation of nature, and the infinite pains anglers have taken to make representations of the segmentations of many of the *Ephemeridæ* by using quill windings for the body would seem to be for naught, except in so far as they affect the artistic eye

of those using them. Many such flies undoubtedly take fish, but I dare say not because
they represent particularly the *colour* of the
natural.

It would seem, therefore, that the most important consideration of the fly-tier who seeks
to imitate the colour of the natural insect should
be the materials to be used. Consequently he
should select only those which are transparent,
or at least translucent, and that reflect the sur-
roundings as readily as the natural insect does as
it floats down-stream on the surface of the water.
It is, of course, quite obvious that the artificial,
no matter how cleverly it may be fashioned,
cannot present the same appearance of translucence as the natural; but one skilfully made
of the appropriate materials will approximate
it nearly enough for all practical purposes. I
believe that the effect produced by reflection of
the colour of the bottom is not so marked upon
an insect resting with its legs upon the surface
and its body above it, as it is upon the insect
with its body directly on the surface. If the
artificial could always be cast so that it rested
only upon its hackle, perhaps the difference between it and the natural would not be so marked.
This may be accomplished, perhaps, by those

anglers who are wedded to fishing the rise, and
who keep their fly absolutely dry until a fish is
seen feeding, but it is asking too much of those
who enjoy seeing their fly upon the water over
likely places.

Although, in certain species of insects which
interest anglers, the difference in size and colour
between the sexes is not great, in others it is
quite marked; and some anglers are of the
opinion that an imitation of the female of a
species is a more killing pattern than one of the
male. A most ingenious explanation of the fish's
preference for the female insect was offered by
the Reverend J. G. Wood in his "Insects at
Home," published in 1871. He says: "Should
the reader be an angler, he will recognise in the
female pseudimago the 'Green Drake,' and in
the perfect insect the 'Grey Drake.' The angler
only cares for the female insects, because the
fish prefer them, laden as they are with eggs, to
the males, which have little in them but air."
The statement certainly endows the trout with
a fine sense of discrimination and taste. That
the female insects are preferred by the trout
may possibly be true, but it is to be regretted
that the author did not explain how he arrived at
the conclusion that they are preferred because

they carry eggs. If he was an angler himself, it was probably the result of personal experience in the use of either the insect or its imitation; or autopsies upon fish may have revealed the fact. In the latter case, the discovery of a preponderating number of females in the stomach of the fish would naturally influence his opinion; but even this discovery could hardly be said to prove that the trout had a preference for the female because it was "laden with eggs." If our author did not fish for trout, his knowledge may have been based either upon information obtained from some angler or upon his own observation of feeding fish; in the latter case, being more of an entomologist than an angler, it is not unreasonable to suppose that his interest was centred upon the insect, and not upon the fish. Having seen a number of females taken in succession—probably at a time when they were predominant—the fact would indicate to his scientific mind a preference for the sex on the part of the fish.

If the fish does in fact prefer the female, the explanation may be found in the life history of the May-fly, which indicates that the male, some time after the sexual function is performed, falls lifeless, while the female, shortly after intercourse,

hovers over the water, and, touching the surface
with that part of her body carrying the now
fertile eggs, deposits them as nature has decreed.
It is this action, made in a succession of dips,
the insect finally resting upon the water, which
presents that appearance of life so attractive to
feeding fish, trout naturally ignoring a dead insect
when their attention is attracted to a fluttering
one.   If trout never took the male insect, nothing
would be gained by imitating it; but they do—
though when they do, it is generally because
there are no interfering females about; or, to
be more gallant, when the more attractive sex
is not strongly in evidence.   It naturally sug-
gests itself to the angler that when the females
of any species are predominant upon the water,
it is advantageous to present a close imitation
of them in colour and size—the form of the
sexes being similar.

It seems to me that the colourist, as a rule, is
much too certain that his flies appear to the
trout as they do to his own sense of sight;
surely, there is no way of demonstrating or es-
tablishing what the truth may be.   Certain it
is that up to the present time, it has not been
possible to fashion an artificial fly that would
give even a faint semblance of the translucence

of the natural insect; and this, it seems to me, is a very important consideration. Using materials available, it is quite impossible to duplicate this delicate appearance of the live insect, and my own conclusion is that materials which will most nearly represent it by permitting a filtering of light are the ones to be employed—preferably materials of quiet tone and colour..

I am of the opinion, also, that the colour, or perhaps the transparency, of the wings of the artificial fly is quite as important as the colour of the body; and I am satisfied, so far as my own angling is concerned, that all erect-winged flies should be tied with wings made of feathers from the starling's wing, or flues from the inside wing feather of the mallard or black duck. For, while trout may not be able to distinguish quite so readily the colour of the wings out of the water as the body of the fly on the water, the natural appearance of the wings may prevent them from scrutinising the body too closely, and thus discovering discrepancies in its colouring; and, while wings of light silvery grey may not appear so to the fish, to my eye they produce a close resemblance to the transparent, gauzy wing common to all of the *Ephemeridæ*, in both the dun and perfect states.

I have a decided preference for winged flies, but that is because they look more like living insects to me when they are on the water than do hackled flies, and not because I think they appear more natural or lifelike to the fish. In practice I have found that hackled flies are taken quite as readily floating as ever they were when I fished them under water, and it may very well be that the hackle fibres standing out from and around the body on and above the surface of the water are even a better imitation of the wings of the *Ephemeridæ* than are the feathers of the winged variety. Certainly a greater amount of light passes through them, and the result may be a better representation of the transparency and neuration of the wings of the natural insect than can be had from the use of artificial wings. At any rate, hackled flies float admirably, and the fish take them freely. And, although the dry fly anglers who use them may feel that something of form and appearance has been sacrificed to utility, their æsthetic sense will probably survive the shock when they find themselves successful—even those who insist that their fly be always beautifully cocked. If it is a consideration to be reckoned with, a hackled fly will outlast a dozen winged ones, being easily dried and humoured back into shape; while, on the other hand, a winged fly is almost hopelessly ruined when taken by a fish. In my own fishing I use a new fly over each fish—an extravagant habit, perhaps—but I love to see a natural looking artificial floating on the water. An old, mussed-up fly may continue to take fish as did the one fly we all have recollections of, that took fish until it was worn to a ravelling, and no other would do; nevertheless, the use of a fresh fly is good insurance against defeat, and, aside from its extravagance, the practice is recommended.

If the angler is to fish with a floating fly, the necessity of some imitation of colour and form is quite evident, but imitation need not be carried to the extent of copying minute variation of colour in slavish detail. To copy the form of the natural fly is, of course, practically impossible. The quantity of hackle used on the artificial to represent the legs of the natural (which number six at most) could hardly be lessened, so great is its aid in floating the fly. Mr. Halford recommends tying the tail of the

artificial in four whisks so as to increase its
buoyancy, even though the setæ of the natural
number but two in most cases—never more than
three. The use of these parts in slightly exagger-
ated form does not denote a contempt for the
keenness of the fish's vision on the part of the
angler employing them. Rather, they are a
necessary evil, and, after all, show a divergence
in form in no way so marked as that occasioned
by the hook.

If approximately exact imitation of form of
the dun or subimago of the *Ephemeridæ* is attempted, the wings of the artificial should be
tied so as to stand close together and directly
upright over the body. But a deviation from
this form to the extent of having the wings
separated will enable the angler to present the
fly cocked more frequently, to drop it lightly,
and will work but little harm.

In my own fishing I am willing to risk any
defeat which a slight variance in colour may in-
vite, if the fly will float erect and in the place I
wish it to. While delicacy in handling the line
will place the fly upright more often than not,
"cocking" the fly is unfortunately not under direct control of the angler. "Cocking" is a very
important part of the imitation of the natural

insect—that imitation described as "position" —but it is not so essential as the accurate and delicate placing of the fly, which last depends entirely upon the skill of the angler. Perhaps "position" is best described by saying that it includes both "attitude" and "plane."

The plane in which the fly is to travel must be selected by the angler, and a combination of the judgment which prompts this selection, and the skill which maintains the plane during a great number of casts, will contribute more to success than the presentation of any particular pattern of fly. As a matter of fact, it is perhaps the only form of imitation which approximates nature—a fly sitting upon the water, being carried down-stream in the same current, and as unhampered and unrestrained in its action as a natural insect. Reliance upon certain patterns purporting to represent certain insects is never so strong again with the angler who, by his own skill, produces an imitation in this way that deludes a good fish. The governing consideration in the practice of this theory of imitation is the selection of the proper current in which to place the fly, and the angler, being guided naturally by his knowledge of the habits of the fish, should make a close study of the trend of the stream currents—particularly of those upon its surface—before beginning operations. Whether or not the fly is to be placed an inch from the bank, or a foot or two away, should depend entirely upon this observation, plane being always the important consideration.

The surface currents carry down numbers of insects, both dead and alive, and the edge of that one which is carrying most drift and is travelling slowest should be chosen by the angler for the delivery of the artificial—always with regard to the avoidance of drag. If there are no insects about or upon the surface of the water, small drift stuff, leaves, twigs, and the like will be carried down in the same plane, and under this surface drift the fish will probably be lying. He is interested in things upon the surface, and it is the angler's business to know it, and to so present the fly that it will come down as naturally as an unhampered insect.

It seems hardly necessary to state that it will be found well-nigh if not quite impossible to imitate the fluttering of a fly over or upon the water, by means of the rod. Yet many of us, when wet fly fishing, have deluded ourselves into the belief that, by the use of a dropper-fly and its careful manipulation, we were simulating, to a certain degree, the fluttering of the natural insect. At any rate, when the fly was taken we flattered ourselves that this was the case. Yet frequently, with the angler's attention centred upon giving to the dropper-fly a proper motion, the submerged tail-fly was taken, and usually by the larger fish. Instead of weakening one's faith in the dropper-fly and the efficacy of its jerky motion, experiences such as these have been known to strengthen a belief in the method; and I have heard the idea expressed that the action of the dropper-fly on the surface had attracted the attention of the fish to the tail-fly. This may be true, but, as a matter of fact, the sunk fly was the better imitation of life, which perhaps accounts for the fish's preference for it.

Those who practised fly fishing in the manner described paid little regard to imitation of colour, and perhaps less to imitation of form; a comparison of the ordinary tackle-shop wet fly with the natural insect will convince any doubting angler that this is so. When they did attempt to imitate the colour of the natural fly, they were accustomed to give little or no thought to colour changes likely to take place upon immersion, with the result that in many cases where silk was used upon the body of the fly, these changes were great enough to destroy almost at once any resemblance to nature the artificial might have had before it was wet. I sometimes find myself believing that these anglers, when they considered colour at all, considered it only in relation to its effect upon their own eyes, and without any regard to the fish's view of it—perhaps not entirely without reason. True, the changes in, or loss of, colour were offset to a considerable extent by the motion, more or less rapid, imparted to the fly, which prevented close scrutiny by the trout, and detection of the fraud. My own notion is that as the fly had to be taken quickly by the fish, if at all, it was taken because it was moving and might be food of some sort and not because it looked like or was an imitation of any particular insect.

There are a great many expert anglers in America who fish with accurate or close imitations of the natural insect, wet or sunk, and who, by virtue of their skill in throwing the fly and their knowledge of the haunts and habits of the trout, are enabled to basket fish of fine

quality and size—fish that would be creditable
to the angler's skill under almost any circumstance of capture. I hazard the opinion, however, that they derive less real sport from their
method than does the angler who fishes with a
single dry and floating fly, imparts no motion
to it, and presents an imitation of a natural
insect which the trout is at liberty to inspect
and, if his suspicion is aroused by the transparency of the fraud or because of some mistake in
delivery, to reject. The dry fly angler must
know quite as much of the haunts and habits
of the fish as the wet fly angler and, to cast his
fly successfully, must have the greater skill.
Above all, the dry fly method is the more fascinating, because the angler actually sees the
rise and the taking of the fly, the sense of sight
as well as the sense of touch conducing to his
pleasurable emotion. His imagination—and all
ardent anglers have imagination—will immediately come into play, and he will find himself
convinced that the imitation has really deceived
the fish into believing that a living insect lay
upon the water.

I venture to suggest the fancy that the taking
of a trout with a nondescript fly of blue or red
—the Parmacheene Belle, the Jenny Lind, or

what-not—even though it may have been presented accurately, superbly cocked and lightly
floating, can never produce in the angler's mind
the feeling of satisfaction that attends him when
he captures a fine fish with a fair imitation
of the natural fly upon the water at the time,
or with one which may be assumed to represent
in colour and form a natural fly of a species
which might be expected to be about at the
season. True, I may seem to be stretching the
point too finely, but I have expressed the fancy
to some of my friends, who, after hearing me,
were good enough to say, as indeed I hoped they
would, "Why, the trout that took the gaudy
fly was a fool fish that would have taken anything." They seemed to believe, as I do, that
the angler who captures a "fool" fish attains
to no honour; that "fool" fish are not the sort
of fish one should covet. The fancy may be
strongly characterised by many as eccentric, I
know, but I am sure that it embodies the principle and spirit of true sportsmanship.

The theory of imitation may not be justly
attacked or lightly set aside because of the fact
that nondescript flies frequently take fish,—
sometimes after fair imitations have been refused. My own belief is that when the highly

coloured nondescript is taken, success should be ascribed to the great skill of the angler and his particularly clean presentation of the fly, or to the fact that the fly was "popped" over and so close to a fish that it was seized because of its proximity.

The taking of trout with either of those two famous flies, the Gold-Ribbed Hare's Ear or the Wickham's Fancy, after fish have refused close imitations of the insects upon which they were feeding, might also be urged as an argument against the imitation theory, though against the colour part of it only, as those two patterns, while imitations, perhaps, of no individual insects, do bear a general resemblance to many, and may be said to be typical in form. It is quite possible that the bright tinsel body of the Wickham's Fancy, and the rib of gold wire or tinsel of the Hare's Ear, represent to the trout that beautiful, iridescent colouring plainly visible upon the body of many natural insects. It is also quite possible that the flashing of the tinsel, opaque though it is, produces that quality of translucence so apparent in the natural insect.

The theory that a counterpart in colour and form of the natural food of the trout is more

likely to prove effective than a nondescript, is
logical, beyond question, not only because the
imitation is likely to delude the fish, but also
because of the appeal it makes to the angler's
own sense of fitness; for it is more than likely
that the angler, knowing his imitation to be a
correct one, will feel a confidence that will enable him to make a cleaner presentation of it,
and to simulate more closely the great essentials
—action and position. And yet within the experience of every angler there have been times
when the very closest imitation of the insect
upon which the trout were presumably feeding,
presented in the best possible manner, has
failed to excite any interest on the part of the
fish, and when an artificial in no way resembling the natural in colour took trout quite as
well as the closest imitation. On such occasions
the faith of the advocate of close imitation
probably received a rude shock.

Although considered out of fashion among
fly fishermen of the present day, one occasionally meets an angler who still adheres to what
is known as the "routine" system. The advocates of this system believe in the necessity of
presenting to the fish a certain series of artificial
flies in February, another series in March, and

continuing a different series for each month of
the season. The theory is based, of course,
upon the imitation of those insects which prevail in the particular months. "Routine" anglers of the past probably had opinions as
firmly fixed as those of anglers of to-day, and
it is very likely that there were a few who persistently clung to the prescribed flies for May,
when fishing that month, and used no others—
fish or no fish.

Whatever effect the colour of the artificial fly
may have upon trout, and however necessary
the proper shade may be felt to be when casting to fish that are feeding upon some particular
species of insect, it is quite certain that the
angler cannot rely upon this form of imitation
alone to take fish. In fishing with the floating
fly the imitation of the form of the natural insect, in my opinion, is quite as essential as that
of its colour, and frequently size will be found
to be even more important than either. My
own experiences have convinced me that imitation of the natural insect is absolutely necessary, and I put the forms this should take
in the following order—the order of their importance:

1st—Position of the fly upon the water.

2nd—Its action.

3rd—Size of the fly.

4th—Form of the fly.

5th—Colour of the fly.

The degrees of importance which separate form, size, and colour may not be widely marked, and, while an exact imitation of the colour, size, and form of the insect which the trout are taking is undoubtedly the ideal combination, I believe that if failure results from any variation from this combination, colour is least responsible for it.   I cannot go so far as to say that trout are entirely colour-blind, or that a correctly sized and shaped artificial dressed in blue would kill a fish that was taking a natural yellow dun, but I do believe that even a great divergence in the shade of colour of the artificial tied in imitation of the natural insect would make no material difference to the fish, if it were properly presented.   In fact, it is my opinion that the artificial need not be yellow at all; that a fly of subdued colour—a Whirling Dun, a Silver Sedge, a Pink Lady, or any fly of similar conformation—will be accepted by the fish feeding upon a little yellow may if its presentation is clean.

We have all had experience with certain fish,

or, perhaps, with many fish, on certain days when, although they appeared to be feeding, it seemed next to impossible to induce a rise. Such failures are invariably ascribed to lack of proper imitation—usually, colour. Sometimes the angler, if he be an expert fly-tier, sets about fashioning a fly which resembles the insect some particular fish is taking, and, presenting it either at that time or the next day, is delighted to find it taken readily. He is immediately a strong advocate of the theory of colour imitation, but he is sometimes uncertain that another pattern would not have served quite as well. Whether or not the pattern did the killing is really an open question.

Just above the dam in front of the Spruce Cabin Inn, at Canadensis, on the Brodhead, is a beautiful stretch of flat water where a great many fine fish may always be found. However, they are not always to be taken. Along the bank opposite the road, which at this point is but a few feet from the stream, is a heavy growth of wood. The rhododendron, which is quite thick, throws its roots out from the bank under water, and the interstices between these roots afford fine hiding-places for the fish. At the upper end of the wood, just where a field joins it, there is a

deep hole which is the home of a very large
trout—a fish that has sorely tried the patience
of the few anglers who have attempted to take
him. An overhanging tree prevents the delivery of a really effective cast from below, and
this undoubtedly accounts for a great many
failures. In three successive years I have raised
this fish seven times (a very small proportion of
the times I have tried for him), on four occasions
leaving my fly with him, and not fastening
solidly on the others. An old tree-stump to
which the fish rushes immediately upon being
hooked accounts for the smashes. The fish will
not rise to a fly on coarse gut, and the fine gut
will not hold him from the stump. If there ever
was a trout that could convince the angler that
exact—and even minute—imitation was absolutely essential, this is the one. He feeds regularly, and may be seen rising steadily for hours
at a time. No amount of casting will put him
down, unless clumsily done, and he will rise
to a natural insect within a few inches of the
artificial, time and again, ignoring the latter
totally. On one occasion—the last time I tried
for him—I failed so signally with all my favourite patterns, that I might have been convinced
that exact imitation was necessary had it not

been for the fact that the fish rose indiscriminately to many different sorts—spinners, gnats, and the smaller members of the beetle family, lady-bugs, and the like, and finally to an artificial which bore no resemblance to any of these. I could not imitate them all, and had tried faithfully with a fair imitation, in size and colour, of one species. It was all to no purpose, however, and to see him continually rising after the many attempts I had made was, to say the least, chastening. I finally decided, after watching him feed for ten minutes, to make one more attempt, and to keep casting the one pattern until he took it or was put down. I knotted on a fly known as the "Mole," which looks like an insect on the water at a distance, but very unlike one when examined closely. This fly was offered probably twenty times or more, without effect, the fish continuing to rise to the natural insects all about it. The cast which eventually raised him differed from any that I had previously made, though without intent on my part. When the fly alighted about a foot above the fish, it fell upon its side with one wing on the surface and the other in the air. Drifting down to within a few inches of the fish, it suddenly stood erect and cocked, this apparently the result of some pressure brought to bear upon the leader by the slow current. It had hardly assumed this upright position, and perhaps was still in the act of regaining its equilibrium, when it disappeared and I was fast to the fish. He added this fly to his collection, and while I sadly examined the leader to ascertain the extent of the damage done, I was not wholly discontented.

I threw a Whirling Dun to this fish one day over a hundred times without putting him down or having him evince the slightest interest in it. A few minutes later, going up-stream from him, I detached the fly from the leader, and, breaking the hook off at the bend, floated it down, and it was taken readily. Perhaps on this occasion I missed the psychological moment, and it is quite possible that the fly would have been taken if I had made one more cast, though not very probable. My own notion of it is that the pattern, when floated down with the hook broken off, had a certain naturalness which was lacking when it was attached to the leader. Either the leader itself was seen, or its restraint upon the fly destroyed its natural appearance. On the other hand, however, the difficulty in presenting the fly because of the overhanging tree may have prevented a proper presentation, though I think a great number of times it approached the fish admirably. Whatever the reason may have been, I did not raise him that day.

Perhaps the actions of another fish that I watched feeding steadily for over an hour may, while hardly offering a solution of the difficulty, present some basis for conjecture. A gentleman who had observed him feeding the day before called my attention to the fact that a good trout occupied a little pocket about one hundred yards above the big fish which has given me so much sport, and he led me mysteriously away from the inn, and as mysteriously up the road, until we reached the spot where the fish was, when he asked me to look in the little eddy and tell him what I saw. For a moment or two I could see nothing but a little drift stuff, but very shortly a good-sized snout broke the surface, and a large bubble floated where it had appeared. While we spent ten or fifteen minutes watching the fish rise, I laid plans to get him the next day. In the morning I thought better of it, however, and planned to crawl down to the water's edge and study his actions at close range. In clambering down the steep bank I

was rather clumsy, and he took fright and disappeared. Getting as close as I could to the water,
I hid behind a bush and watched for the fish to
return, which he did in just four minutes, timed
by my watch. This in itself was interesting, as
it tended to show how long the incident lingered
in his memory. The eddy which he occupied
was formed at the bottom of a rather swift little
run by a large boulder that deflected a part of
the stream toward the bank and started it up-
stream again. The fish stationed himself exactly in the centre of this up-stream current,
which was not very strong, and immediately
began feeding. He rose three or four times a
minute, sometimes oftener, according to the opportunities presented. There were very few
insects in the air, but apparently a great many
upon the surface of the water. I think perhaps
a half dozen or so of different sorts alighted directly in the eddy, all of which the fish accounted
for, but the majority of rises were to insects
that were carried down-stream upon the surface,
and collected in the eddy. They were of all
sizes and shapes, from the tiniest *Diptera*, which
interested him much, to a small, dead butterfly,
lying flat, which he examined closely, but de-
clined. It was this discrimination that puzzled

me. He took many apparently dead insects, and refused many. He never refused any that were alive, and size or colour or shape made no difference to him. Why some dead insects appealed to him and others did not, I cannot guess, unless, perhaps, those that appeared dead to me did not look so to him. Every time he rose, it was with the greatest deliberation; never did he rush at the fly, and once when a particularly active dun fluttered on the surface close to him, instead of rushing for it as I expected him to do, he merely backed up under it, rising very slowly, finally sucking it in. Another thing I noticed was that he never went forward to take an insect. He went forward frequently to meet one, but always took it backing up. This manner of taking a fly is not at all unusual, as fish may frequently be seen backing under an artificial, sometimes even turning down-stream before taking it. If an insect showed the slightest activity, which many of them did in various ways, moving the body up and down, opening and closing their wings, or moving their legs, he never hesitated, but took it at once, even the tiniest. If the insect lay upon its side, he would drift with it a foot or two, sometimes taking it, frequently leaving it. On one occasion he backed under an insect in this position for a distance of about three feet, and stopped, apparently abandoning it; but the next instant he turned, took it quietly, and swam slowly back to his station. I was unable to see this insect as clearly as I wished, and I do not know that it moved at the moment it was taken, but from the manner in which the fish took the others, it seems likely that this was the case. Notwithstanding the decided preference shown by this fish for the moving or living insects, he rose and took a piece of a twig about three eighths of an inch long which I flipped to him at a moment when he was unoccupied, and I found this twig in his stomach the next day, together with three spruce needles, two of which were green and one yellow. Would the presence of this drift stuff in his stomach indicate that the fish was nearsighted, or that such drift really had a place in his dietary?

I have found in the stomachs of trout many small sticks, plainly fresh, and which certainly formed no part of a caddis casing. Why they were taken is hard to say; some anglers have expressed the opinion, which may possibly be sound, that the fish are compelled to take them in the attempt to secure some poor shipwrecked insects which are using them as rafts. I prefer

to believe, however, that they are mistaken by
the fish for some form of life, perhaps having
the appearance of caddis larvæ. The spruce
needles were probably mistaken for willow flies,
or some of the family of *Perlidæ*—those with
wings that fold along the back.

That the fish was taken the following morning on the Mole, which certainly imitated no
insect with which he may have been familiar,
perhaps means nothing. As he was feeding
regularly, and rather indiscriminately, he was
probably an easy fish to take. The Mole was
just another morsel that looked natural enough.
The first cast took him, the fly drifting up to
him after having been cast over the boulder at
the bottom of the eddy. The leader was not
seen, and as the fly appeared in a natural, upright position, his suspicion was not aroused,
and a minute or two later he was in the net.
Withal, the fish showed a decided preference for
living insects, and refused those which were certainly no deader than an artificial fly; and yet
the Mole was taken with just as much confidence as if it had been a living thing. I think
it quite within reason that any pattern of fly
properly presented would have taken the fish
as readily as did the fly which he rose to, and
my conclusion is that it was because of its

position that it was taken. My observation of this fish confirmed my belief in the necessity of so placing the fly that it would come to the fish just as a natural insect would, floating upon the surface. There is a great difference between the effect produced by a fly cast upon likely looking water, or to a feeding fish, without special care as to where it may alight, and that produced by one cast exactly to the proper spot.

The larger fish down-stream apparently was interested only in live insects, which is shown, I think, by his utter refusal of every artificial of any pattern, including the Mole, which he ignored each time it came over him, until the twist in the leader, or some other uncontrolled action, turned the fly over on the surface, and simulated to a certain extent the struggle of an insect endeavouring to rise from the water. I am convinced that my many failures with this fish were due, in the main, to my inability to place the fly in a proper position. This conclusion is supported, I think, by the fact that he took the unattached Whirling Dun—which I was careful to float down to him in the proper current—after he had refused it scores of times when attached to the leader.

CHAPTER VI

SOME FANCIES—SOME FACTS

SOME anglers have come to believe that the trout of our heavily fished streams have developed such wariness and cunning that they view the artificial fly of the angler with suspicion, even if they do not actually know it to be an imitation. In the light of certain experiences of my own, I am unable to concur in the conclusion reached by these anglers that trout are capable of reasoning or remembering specific incidents for any long period of time; it is my opinion—presented, however, with some hesitancy—that they refuse the artificial fly not because they have had previous experience with it but because of various other reasons, the most important of which are the unnatural *action* of the fly and the probability of the fish having seen the angler, his rod, the leader, or the shadow of one or all. Surely the trout of these streams cannot in July and August remember the hordes of anglers that invaded their haunts in May. Admitting it to be true that in the earlier months of the season it is comparatively easy to take trout, even when the streams are full of anglers, and that later, in the summer months, with but two or three anglers, or at most a half dozen, to be seen, infinite skill is often required to induce even a single fair rise, something other than the memory of the fish must be the cause of his reluctance to rise, as the following instances may tend to prove.

In July, 1911, I rose, hooked, and returned to the water four fish three times each in one week; and these fish were taken in the same place and on the same pattern of fly each time. On another occasion I rose and landed an eleven-inch rainbow trout which I returned to the water, and the next day this fish was brought home by a fellow angler who had taken him in the same place. This last may possibly have been another fish; but about the four other trout there can be no mistake, as I marked them without injury before returning them to the water the first time. I was prompted to make this experiment after taking a fish from one spot, which resembled closely in size and form a fish I had returned to the water a few days previously. This fish was one of the four, and was twice taken and returned. Each of the fish gave up a minute piece of its caudal fin in return for its life.

Often, too, one hears of trout being taken with the fly of some luckless or careless angler fast in its jaw. On the Brodhead, in 1907, one morning about eight o'clock, I rose and killed a native trout weighing about a pound, which had a fly in its lip left there by an angler the evening before; his nose was raw and bleeding where he had scraped it against the stones in his efforts to dislodge the hook. Experiences of this sort do not tend to confirm the belief that fish have memory.

The more enemies an animal has the more wary it is, and in those least able to defend themselves against attack the senses which enable them to avoid danger are most keen. In some animals, sight, smell, and hearing are all keenly alert; in others a combination of two of these senses is relied upon, and in rare cases but one. These faculties give warning of the approach of an enemy, and time, in most cases, for the use of such secondary means of defence as are provided by nature—speed, flight, protective colouring, or whatever they may be.

In the case of trout, since scientists have come to no definite conclusion that fish can smell, we may safely assume—from the fly fisher's standpoint, at any rate—that this sense has no place in our study. The same may be said of taste and feeling; the luckless fish relying upon these senses would find himself hard and fast before he could reach the conclusion that the feathered fly was not what it appeared to be. This leaves sight and hearing as the means by which the trout is apprised of the approach of danger—and the angler may well say that they are quite sufficient.

> "If fish could hear as *well* as see,
> Never a fisher would there be."

The experiments made by Ronalds and described in his "Fly Fishers' Entomology" prove more or less conclusively that trout cannot hear, or at least are not disturbed by sounds produced in the air. Now, while it is quite certain that they are affected by vibrations communicated to the water, the bottom of the stream, or its banks, I do not believe that the disturbance is conveyed to the senses of the fish unless the vibrations take place close to it. In this connection, an experiment made by myself may prove interesting, even though it may be in no way conclusive, as it was tried but once, and the trout which served as the medium may have been "deaf." Taking my position on a high bank above the fish and completely out of sight, I had a young man go below and thirty feet downstream. Lying prone upon the opposite shore, which was level with the water, and taking pains not to make any quick move which might have spoiled the experiment, he took two stones, one in each hand, and, at a signal from me, struck them together, a foot under water. He did this a dozen times, each succeeding blow being harder than the previous one. The sound produced by the clashing stones had no apparent effect upon the fish, but I noticed that the series of small waves or ripples created by the disturbance of the surface, upon reaching the trout, seemed to make it uneasy, and it began "weaving" from side to side, covering, however, not more than a foot in its movements. When the fish had quieted down, and after another trial, with the same effect, I had the lad abandon the stones and make as large a wave as he could, directed toward the fish. There was considerable splashing during the attempt, but the trout gave no indication that it was aware of the disturbance until the first ripple was passing over it, when it became as uneasy as before, and

even more excited; and not until the ripple
had ceased did it resume the almost stationary
position previously held. The fish was about
one foot from the surface, and the largest ripple
not over two inches in height; consequently, its
motion could hardly have been felt at a depth
greater than six inches; yet the fish was disturbed—whether by the action of the water itself or by the shadow cast by the ripple, I leave
for the reader to decide. Of one thing I am
positive: the fish was not disturbed by the
sound of the colliding stones.

The fish's sense of sight is so keen that it
alone enables the trout to avoid danger, and is
absolutely necessary to its existence. But it is
not so keen, in my opinion, as to enable the
trout to detect minute differences between the
angler's fly and the natural insect—except, of
course, when the action of the artificial fly is so
unnatural as to warn the fish, or frighten it.

Adherents to the theory that trout are able
to distinguish between the angler's artificial
fly and the natural insect, make much of the
admitted fact that a fish is rarely taken from
the much fished Southern streams on a Parmacheene Belle or other nondescript. There
is a great deal of truth in the contention; but

the fact is lost sight of that these flies are usually presented by anglers who have but little
knowledge of the habits of the fish they are seeking, their experience having been gained solely
at the expense of the trout of the wilderness.

While not asserting the opinion that a gaudy
fly will not take fish, I would remind the reader
that such a fly is usually cast by a man who
presents himself to the fish before he offers the
fly—with the inevitable result. The instinct of
self-preservation is strong in the trout, and he
flees the apparition, though, if he would but
realise it, he was never safer than at the very
moment of its appearance.

Anything unusual that comes within the
vision of the fish means to him a possible
danger, and the desire to feed, if he be in the
mood, is forgotten in his effort to locate the
point of attack. Any shadow thrown upon the
water indicates the approach of an enemy—
a heron, a kingfisher, a mink (the most destruc-
tive of all), or a man, in whom he recognises an
enemy only because he sees a moving object.
Beset as the trout is at all times, it is but natural
that he should make use of his only means of
defence—speed—and escape while he may. On
streams that are much fished, frequent sight

of man is afforded the fish, and, although the
actions of the angler (except in rare cases) do
not indicate the danger of actual personal en-
counter, the fish retires, precipitately or quietly,
according to the manner in which he is approached. It is this sight of man or his shadow,
and not the the ability to detect the fraud, that
impels him to refrain from taking the fly. If
the angler remain hidden from view, and throw
the fly properly, without the accompaniment of
shadows of himself, rod, line, or leader, and a
rise is not induced, he may safely assume that
it is lack of inclination on the part of the fish,
and not a contempt for the pattern of the fly,
bred of familiarity with it, that causes him to
refuse it.

These facts, or fancies, as they may be considered, are presented only as they may support a theory that accounts for the wariness and
cunning of the trout of much fished streams,
and the apparent lack of these attributes in the
trout of the wilderness. It is a well known fact
that a man who wishes to take trout in Maine,
Quebec, New Brunswick, Nova Scotia, or, in fact,
anywhere in the north woods where they are
plentiful, need have had no previous experience
to enable him to catch all that the law, or his

conscience, permits. This same man fishing in
Pennsylvania or lower New York, practising
the same methods he applied in the North, will
leave the streams with the idea firmly fixed in
his mind that they are barren of fish, or, per-
chance, viewing the catch made by a more
skilful angler, will come to the conclusion that
the fish are more wary than their fellows of the
North, and that a skill unknown to the angler
lacking experience on these waters is required
to take them. The instinct of self-preservation
is quite as strong in the trout of the wilderness,
but expresses itself in other ways that are in
keeping with the different conditions they have
to contend with.

In most places where trout are plentiful,
there is abundance of room for them to
escape from an enemy, an advantage denied
the trout which are restricted to the narrow
confines of one of our mountain streams, particularly when the water is low and the trout
have to be more wary than ever, if they are to
survive. While endowed with the same agility
and the same keenness of sight, the wilderness
fish are emboldened by numbers, and appear to
depend a great deal upon one another for warning; they are alert only to the "main chance";

i. e., the taking of anything that looks like food. This explains why it is easy for the veriest tyro fishing in the wilderness to take as many fish with the fly in a single day as the expert on the Southern streams would be content to take in a season. Many of these big catches are made upon lakes and streams that are heavily fished; yet the angler rarely has to resort to methods which require any great skill. In many instances the fishing is done from a canoe, and fish are taken quite close to it, the interest on the part of the trout seemingly being actuated by nothing more than a desire to "beat his fellows to it."

The law of "the survival of the fittest" applies equally to the fish of the Southern streams and to the fish of the wilderness. In both cases vigilance and agility are the price of continued existence—on the one hand, to avoid the attack which may deprive the fish of life, on the other, to excel in the scramble for that which will sustain it.

If the old saw which runs, "When the wind is in the north the skilful fisherman goes not forth," etc., referred to fly fishing, it was plainly meant for the angler who did not care to indulge in his sport when the chilling blasts from this quarter were howling about the stream,

because it is in no sense descriptive of the effect
of the wind upon the feeding of the fish. When
an angler has taken trout under conditions
ranging from flat calms to gales from every
point of the compass, it is difficult for him to
believe that wind has any direct effect upon the
fish, aside, perhaps, from the influence it exerts
in promoting or retarding the development of
the insects upon which they feed; and this last
depends more upon the temperature of the wind
than it does upon its force or the quarter from
which it comes.

The angler who is fishing the flat, still water
of a pond or lake hopes for a breeze in order
that he may take advantage of the ripple caused
by it, and deceive or approach his fish more
readily. The advantage afforded by the breeze
is offset on many occasions, in proportion to the
force of the wind, by the increased difficulty of
casting; and when a stiff wind is blowing down-
stream or in the face of the angler it is of negli-
gible value. So far as comfort is concerned, a
chilling wind is very disagreeable, and the angler unfortunate enough to be upon the stream
during a "norther" in the early spring is quite
of the mind that trout are sensible of it, when
he finds them in no keener mood for the sport

than he is; yet it was just such a day, as cold
and blustering as I have ever experienced, that
the trout on the Brodhead, of which I have told,
rose to the fly which was made to play such
pranks by the wind.

There is a gentleman of my acquaintance, an
expert with the fly, who holds that it is useless
to fish a wooded stream when the wind is blowing heavily, not so much because of any change
in atmospheric conditions, but because the rapidly moving shadows thrown upon the water
by the frantically waving overhead limbs and
branches seem to make the trout restless or
nervous, and unwilling to feed. Be this as it
may, it certainly does not apply upon the open
stretches, for there the wind is of distinct advantage, because the ruffled surface helps to
conceal the angler's activities from the fish.
When success does not attend the caster's
efforts on days of this sort, failure must be
ascribed to his state of mind rather than to the
condition of the weather.

And here just a hint from my own experience: beware of fishing in big woods on a very
windy day; dead limbs may come crashing down
at any moment. On one occasion a difference of
ten feet in my position would have meant dis-

aster and these pages might never have been written.

During periods of high wind the trout are often treated to a change of diet, land flies, grasshoppers, and beetles, unhappily overcome, being readily and cheerfully accepted. On one occasion, all the trout killed by five or six anglers disclosed the fact, upon autopsy, that potato-bugs had formed a large part of their food that morning; and a fly which resembled this beetle only in size and shape was found very effective. This fly was a herl-bodied brown palmer, called the Marlow Buzz.

The many anglers who still hold to the belief that trout will not rise during a thunder-storm do so, no doubt, because it offers an excuse for retiring from the stream and seeking shelter,— for which they cannot be blamed. It is not the pleasantest situation to be caught in one of the vicious storms which sometimes break with scant warning. If, however, it happens that the angler is so placed that he is far from a road or path that will lead him to some cover, he is far safer in the streams than in the woods; and, making the best of a bad bargain, he should continue his fishing. In all likelihood, he will come to the conclusion that the theory is not founded upon fact; for, while trout do not invariably rise during thunder-storms, they may be taken on occasions when the reverberations are so heavy as to be felt almost as distinctly as they are heard—the effect upon the fish not being apparent.

If the storm be accompanied by a heavy rain, dry fly fishing ceases as soon as the water begins to rise and becomes discoloured, because, even though the fish may be ready to feed, there is small likelihood of the angler's fly being seen by them through the discoloured water. But no time should be wasted in returning to the stream after the flood has run off and the water is clearing, as the opportunity for taking fish is then probably the best that will be presented.

Idiosyncrasy—or shall we call it superstition? —seems to enter into the make-up of a great many anglers.

Squire Jake Price, now dead, father of the boys who keep that comfortable hostelry on the Brodhead, at Canadensis, in Pennsylvania, well known to many anglers, was famous as a trout fisherman. He fished with the fly only, tied his own flies, and from the time his sons were able to wade the streams would permit them to use nothing else. Always keen to be at his fishing, he would not be dragged to the waterside unless his "almanac" told him the time was propitious. Curiously enough, when he did go, he always took fish; but this may be ascribed to the fact that he "knew how" rather than to a revelation from the zodiac.

A story is told of an angler of indifferent skill, but anxious to take home a basket of fish, who induced Squire Jake to accompany him one morning. He felt certain of getting trout, the Squire having approved of the day. Upon their arrival at the stream-side he proceeded to line his creel with fine grasses and ferns, when, to his amazement, the Squire left abruptly, saying he could not fish with one who would thus "fly in the face of Providence." Was this superstition, or only anger at the other's assurance?

Of similar mind to the Squire are those anglers who persist in carrying, to their own inconvenience, a diminutive creel and smaller net, preferring to cram into either a fish twice too large rather than to carry equipment of adequate size; the taking of a good fish is a circumstance which they feel may never be realised if they anticipate it.

Some consideration must be given to the belief of those who have unbounded faith in a particular pattern of fly. There are wet fly fishermen on the Beaverkill who never make up their cast of three flies without including the Royal Coachman; and at least one of these, whom I know, uses this fly, dry, in preference to any other. While the pattern has no place in my book, I respect the faith others have in it, which faith, however, is often rudely shaken—for a short period, at least. After fishing carefully for hours with his favourite fly without response, the angler meets a brother angler who displays two or three nice fish taken on the Queen, the Bumble, or what not, and passes on. For the nonce the favourite is discarded, the Queen or Bumble is knotted on, but the result is the same—nothing. Another pattern is tried—same result. Again the fly is changed, and again, and still again. In his anxiety our friend uses little skill, less judgment, and lacks entirely the great essential—faith.

Many times an angler, stepping quietly into the stream at the beginning of his day's sport, casts his fly to a spot where his experience tells him a trout may be, and meets with response almost immediately. His next cast is accepted quite as quickly, and in these few delicious moments, with the nucleus in his creel, the vision he has had of the one great day's catch begins to take tangible form. But how rudely the vision is dissipated in the next four or five hours, during which time he gets not a single rise!

There are other anglers in whom entirely different emotions are aroused when they are successful in taking fish soon after their arrival at the stream. To them this incident spells utter failure for the rest of the day. It seems to me that these men neglect to analyse the situation, permitting superstition to run riot with reason, and, to my mind, their troubles may be ascribed to any one of three causes: (1) At the time the angler first steps into the stream he may be arriving at the top or at the end of a rise that started fifteen, twenty, or thirty minutes before, which short space of time may be responsible for the difference between two fish and a possible half dozen. If the angler meets with this experience during the season when the water is very low and clear, and the day hot and bright, he may be satisfied that, to a great extent, such is the explanation. But, if he is not a principal to cause number two, he should be able to continue taking some trout, even under these trying conditions. (2) The

optimist arriving at the stream side prepares
his rod, surveys the scene of action, and, having
selected the spot he is to fish, enters the stream
some distance below, and quietly proceeds to
his point of vantage. Every instinct alert, he
is careful to make no mistake, and his care and
deftness are at once rewarded. Continuing a
few yards, another fish is taken, and possibly a
bit farther on, still another. Then, blinded by
conceit, he falls into the pit he has dug for himself. He thinks he has at last the right medi-
cine, and unknowingly (and unmeaningly, bless
his heart) there steals over him a feeling akin to
contempt for the wary fish he is after. The next
pool is approached with a swagger that fills the
trout that inhabit it with consternation, and
drives all thought of feeding from them. Some
day it will occur to this angler that he has been
a bit overconfident, and he will try getting out
of the stream, going up a hundred yards through
the brush, and starting all over as at the beginning; then he will come to a realisation of
the truth. (3) The pessimist, by analysing
cause number two, may overcome, to a certain
extent, the deep-rooted superstition that, because he gets a trout easily at the outset, he will
get no more throughout the day. His is a state

of mind that surely is not conducive to best effort. After taking a fish on the first few casts, his subsequent proceedings are governed by an anomalous condition of mind—he believes that his sport is over, yet hopes the day may prove the fallacy of his theory, and, in an unconscious effort to avoid his fate, he fishes in a careless manner.

The rise which indicates that a large fish is feeding has, upon the minds of some anglers, a psychological effect which works toward defeating any attempt they make in throwing to him. The angler is alert only to the necessity of placing his fly near the fish, and, caution thrown to the winds, he approaches in a manner which might be called stealthy if he used it in escaping from a burning building. Having begun without cautioning, thus preparing the way to dismal failure, he fixes his eye upon the spot where the rise was noted, and sends his fly, with no thought, perhaps, other than to get it on the water as quickly as possible. If his efforts meet with no reward—and the chances are that they will not—and many fish are to be seen feeding all about, he probably becomes frantic with desire to take one, runs through a rapid change of flies in the hope of finding one that will entice, wastes many precious minutes in his fumbling uncertainty, when suddenly all rising ceases, and he has lost his opportunity.

The remedy for all of these cases is the same —calmness and deliberation.

The suggestion that the sight of the leader is abhorrent to trout brings up a point upon which great stress is laid by dry fly anglers. That the fish is warned off by seeing the gut upon the surface of low, clear water is to my mind more certain than anything else in the sport of angling. Whether or not frequent sight of the leader makes the fish familiar with it, is difficult to determine. Personally, I believe that when a fish refuses a fly because he has seen the leader attached to it, his timidity is likely to be due to the impression of its unnaturalness at the moment, rather than to his recollection of having seen a like object before and learned its danger. In plain words—probably inviting a storm of protest and criticism—I am not inclined to the notion that trout become "educated" on streams that are much fished. These trout are quite sensitive to danger, but, in my opinion, only imminent danger affects them. The sudden appearance of an angler waving a rod, or of a cow fording the stream, are disturbing to trout, one just as much as the other. Both angler and cow are in motion, and that alone attracts the eye of the fish; both intercept light, and thus cast shadows upon the water, which mean possible danger to him.

Anything falling upon the surface of the water arouses interest on the part of a fish observing it; if it be a shadow, he suspects danger in proportion to its size and activity; the fall of a leaf, a twig, or an insect is interesting to him in one way or another. Frequently a leaf or twig, if not so large as to frighten him at once, will be investigated at close range. I have thrown maple buds to trout, which were taken almost immediately upon striking the water, being slowly ejected afterward when it was discovered that the buds were not food.

An insect intercepts light, but the insignificant shadow it casts does not alarm the fish, and his attention is directed to the insect alone. When the artificial fly is thrown, however, it must necessarily be with the leader attached, and if it so happens that the leader, or that part of it close to the fly, *floats upon the surface*, the attention of the fish is divided between the fly itself and the leader, the latter standing out boldly between the eye of the fish and the background of sky.   The leader floating upon the surface is more visible to the fish than when fully submerged.   The angler who wishes to demonstrate this may do so by placing a length of gut upon the surface of some still, sunlit water, noting the shadow cast by it upon the bed of the stream, and then comparing it with the shadow of the same gut submerged.

The water-strider, skipping nimbly over the surface of clear, shallow water, affords an excellent illustration of shadow effects.   The shadows thrown upon the bottom by this curious insect are enormous when compared with its actual size, and those resulting from the depression in the surface made by the insect's feet look to be as big as a dime.   It was observation of the shadows thrown by the water-strider that prompted me to experiment with the leader; and my first attempt, made with the lightest leader I had, produced a shadow upon the bottom *nearly an inch in width*.   Whether or not this shadow alarms the fish more than does the leader itself, probably depends upon the circumstances controlling the direction of his attention at the time, but it is certain that one or the other does have a marked effect upon his behaviour.   Perhaps both combined have, and, consequently, he can hardly be expected to take the fly when his interest is divided betwixt the desire to feed, on the one hand, and suspicion tinged with fear on the other.

Upon glassy water, the glistening leader, twisting and turning upon the surface, accompanied by little wrinkles along its entire length, presents to the fish an aspect which must at least arouse his curiosity and distract his attention from the fly—even though it does not terrify him and scare him off entirely.

The visibility of the leader has always been one of the problems of the fly fisher, irrespective of the question of drag. Many attempts have been made to produce a leader of neutral colour that would be invisible, or approximately so, when on the water. I have done some experimenting in this direction myself. I have tried all colours—greens and browns, mist colours and greys. I have steeped leaders in ink until they came out absolutely black. Yet, withal, I have failed to satisfy myself that one was better than the others, when I came to use it on the stream. If there is one colour that a leader may be stained to render it less visible than another, I do not know what it is. I am inclined to believe, however, that gut of natural colour is less conspicuous than gut that has been coloured to make it harmonise with the water. Partial solutions of the problem may be had by assuming certain controlling conditions to exist. For instance, as the fish views the leader from below, and against a background formed by the sky, a light-blue leader to harmonise with the background on a bright day, or, for a similar reason, a grey one on a cloudy day, may be the very thing. Of course, it is all very speculative, because the main element of the problem—what the fish thinks—is an unknown one.

In my opinion, the floating, drifting leader, with its wrinkles and its convolutions, constitutes the worst possible form of "drag," which must be avoided if trout are to be taken where the water is slow and unruffled. The angler should endeavour to have the fly float and the leader sink—obviously, by keeping one *dry* and the other *wet*. He will find it even more difficult to keep the leader wet than to keep the fly dry; even when thoroughly saturated, the former will not submerge readily when the fly is thrown as lightly as it should be.

In swifter water it is easier to keep the leader under the surface, but here one encounters another form of drag which, while in my opinion

not so fatal to the angler's chances as the one I
have described, is oftentimes more exasperating.
This form of drag takes place when the fly,
although accurately and lightly placed in the
desired spot, is snatched away almost at once
by the current pulling on the line or leader; the
fish may thus be deprived of an opportunity of
securing the fly, or he may refuse it because of
its unnatural action. The natural insect, unhampered by any "string to it," drifts naturally
with the current, and the feeding fish which
makes for it, having accurately judged its position and pace, rarely misses. The artificial,
when drag is exerted upon it, dashes down-stream
at a speed always greater than that of the
current in which it is; besides the unnatural
action it acquires, it sometimes ceases to be a
floating fly, being dragged under the surface by
the pull of the line or leader in the swifter water.
Drag of this sort usually occurs when the line
or the leader must fall on the swift water between the angler and the spot he desires to
reach with the fly, and is not always avoidable.
Where possible, the line and leader should be
kept out of the swift water.

When casting to the eddies at the head of a
pool, the angler should assume a position on the

same side of the current as the eddy to be fished. An effort should be made to place the line in the water that is turning *up-stream* where the eddy begins to take form. The fly falling farther up will remain floating for a time—quite long enough to be taken by a fish. If this eddy cannot be reached from directly below, because of the depth of water or on account of some obstacle to clean casting, the fly may be thrown across the current with the up-stream curve in the leader. Where this is found necessary the leader should be watched carefully and, before it begins to exert a pull on the fly, the latter should be retrieved quickly. The fly may be taken from the water quietly, as it should be, if a forward loop is thrown in the line similar to that used in the switch cast. This action removes the leader from the water with but little disturbance, and, as the fly is about to leave the surface, the backward cast will carry it clear, practically without commotion. In the same manner an eddy across stream may be fished with little danger of a fish being put down by the sight of a dragging fly. The method, however, calls for keen alertness, and the angler must have perfect and constant control of rod and line.

Swift water in either a rift or a run should have no terrors for the angler who fears a dragging fly, if he will first study the currents. Even if he feels that a fish is occupying water that can be reached only by risking drag, he must always bear in mind that a fish is more likely to come some distance to a natural-looking fly than it is to take an unnatural one close to it. A spot should be selected as close to the assumed position of the fish as possible; but this choice should always be guided by the necessity for placing the fly on water swifter than that in which the line and leader will fall. The "retarded" drag which may set in after the fly has been placed in swift water, has floated downstream until it is below the leader, and is held back by it, need not be feared, because the fly will have covered a considerable stretch in its travel, and may then be retrieved. Sometimes the sight of a dragging fly is more offensive to the angler than it is to the fish; and there are occasions when it will be taken, if its actions have not been particularly rude.

As an aid to keeping the line afloat in swift water, an application of deer's fat, or one of the many preparations now made for the same purpose, is recommended. It is sufficient to treat three or four yards at the end of the line, and the dressing should be rubbed down smoothly afterward. Under no circumstances should any dressing be applied to the leader, because, even though it helps to float the fly, the gut will be found to be annoyingly buoyant when the still reaches are being fished, and will produce that troublesome form of drag already described, and which I consider the only form that unduly taxes the ingenuity and patience of the expert and even-tempered. My own opinion is that the sight of the leader does not seriously deter the fish from taking the fly in swift water. But on smooth water a superbuoyant leader is a nuisance and a plague and an abomination.

CHAPTER VII

THE POINT OF VIEW

THE capture of a splendid ouananiche under circumstances most trying is somewhere described by a well-known writer, who, in his inimitable style, exhibits himself before his readers running through his entire assortment of artificial flies, first one and then another and still another, and all without avail. We see him casting, casting, all impatience, determined, perhaps exasperated. Surely some sort of lure is predicated. But what? Ah, he has it! A live grasshopper. Then follows the pursuit, the overtaking, and the capture of the grasshopper, the impaling of its unfortunate body, its proffer to the fish, a desperate battle, and, finally, the contemplation of the finest fish of the season safely landed. The thrilling moment! Which was it? Why, of all moments, that one in which he captured the grasshopper! The story affords a fine illustration of what I call the "point of view," but until after the revelation that came to me with my first success with the dry fly, I did not fully appreciate its finer and deeper meanings.

Certain pleasurable excitement always attends the taking of a good fish by the true angler. Yet, after all, the quality of his gratification should be measured by the method of capture. In angling, as in all other arts, one's taste and discrimination develop in proportion to his opportunity to see, study, and admire the work of greater artists. Even as a knowledge of the better forms of music leads, eventually, to a distaste for the poorer sorts, and as familiarity with the work of great painters leads to disgust with the chromolithograph-like productions of the dauber, so, too, does a knowledge of the higher and more refined sorts of angling lead just as surely to the ultimate abandonment of the grosser methods. One who has learned to cast the fly seldom if ever returns to the days when he was content to sit upon the bank, or the string-piece of a pier, dangling his legs overboard while he watched his cork bobbing up and down, indicating by its motions what might be happening to the bunch of worms at the hook end of the line; and, even as casting the fly leads to the abandonment of the use of bait, so, too, does the dry fly lead to the abandonment of the wet or sunk fly. There can be no question but that the stalking of a rising trout bears to the sport of angling the same relation to its grosser forms as the execution of a symphony bears to the blaring of the local brass band. It appeals to the higher and more æsthetic qualities of the mind, and dignifies the pot-hunter's business into an art of the highest and finest character.

I am thus brought to the consideration of the pot-hunter and the fish hog. Many angling writers there be who have not hesitated, nor have they been ashamed, to describe the taking of great numbers of trout on separate and many occasions. They feel, no doubt, that such narratives entitle them to consideration as authorities on the subject. I quote from one—who shall be nameless—his bragging description of a perfect slaughter of fish. After telling of twenty-five or thirty trout taken during midday, naming at least a dozen flies he had found *killing*, he concludes: "All my trout were taken from the hook and *thrown twenty-five* feet to shore. Thirty, my friend claimed, yet when I came to count tails I found *forty* as handsome trout as ever man wished to see, and all caught from six in the evening until dark, about seven forty-five. I had no net or creel, therefore had to lead my trout into my hand. The friend at whose house I was staying claims I lost more than I caught by having them flounder off the hook *while trying to take them by the gills and by flinging them ashore."* The italics are mine. And this fellow had the temerity to add that some poor devil (an itinerant parson, he called him) annoyed him by wading in and fishing with a "stick cut from the forest." Had Washington Irving witnessed this fellow's fishing I doubt that he would have been moved to write: "There is certainly something in angling that tends to produce a gentleness of spirit and a pure serenity of mind."

There are men calling themselves anglers!— save the mark—who limit the number of fish to the capacity of creel and pockets, and to whom size means merely compliance with the law—a wicked law, at that, which permits the taking of immature trout. It is not an inspiring sight to see a valiant angler doing battle with a six-inch trout, and, after brutally subjecting it to capture, carefully measuring it on the butt of his rod which he has marked for the purpose, stretching it, if necessary, to meet the law's requirements, and in some cases, if it does not come up to the legal standard, rudely flinging it away in disgust—to die as a result of its mishandling. Happily, this tribe is not increasing, because of the persistent efforts of true sportsmen who do not hesitate to denounce it publicly whenever opportunity arises. Perhaps it is permissible to hope that the pot-hunter and the fish hog may in time disappear, but, if this desirable end is to be brought about, true sportsmen must not shun their duty but must wage unceasing war against them.

Books on angling abound in word-pictures descriptive of the strenuous battle of the hooked fish to escape its captor, many such pictures being so vividly drawn that the reader fairly imagines himself in the writer's waders, his excitement ending only when the captive is in the net. It is meet, therefore, that some consideration be given to the point of view of those anglers who believe that great merit attaches to him who lands a good fish on light tackle.

There can be no question of the excitement attending the playing of a good trout nor of the skill required in its handling, and this excitement, in proportion to the ideas of the individual, is a greater or less measure of the sport; but, given the opportunity, it is my opinion that, in the hands of a skilful angler, the rod will kill nine out of ten fish hooked. Be that

as it may, can the degree of skill, even with the
lightest tackle, displayed in the landing of a
two or three pound trout (a fine fish on our
Eastern streams) bear comparison with that
required in the capture of a six-foot tarpon on
a six-ounce rod and a six-strand line? A six-
foot tarpon will weigh about one hundred and
twenty pounds, and the line will bear a dead-
weight strain of twelve pounds. Compare this
with the three-pound trout taken on a gut leader,
the weakest link in the angler's chain, which
will lift a weight of two or more pounds, and
the futility of beguiling oneself with the belief
that the trout has any advantage will be apparent.

The playing of a trout is undeniably part of
the sport, but, however difficult one wishes to
make it, it is but secondary to the pleasure de-
rived from casting the fly and deluding that old
trout into mistaking it for a bit of living food.
It is this art, this skill, this study of the fish itself and its habits, that places dry fly fishing
for trout far ahead of all other forms of angling.
It has been said that there is no sport that requires in its pursuit a greater knowledge of
the game, more skill, more perseverance, than
fly fishing, and that no sport holds its votaries

longer. I am quite of this opinion. "There is no genuine enjoyment in the easy achievement of any purpose," and in fly fishing a full measure of satisfaction is obtained only when the taking of a single fish is accomplished under conditions most difficult and trying.

The true angler is content only when he feels that he has taken his fish by the employment of unusual skill. The highest development of this skill at the present state of the angler's art is the dry fly method. I do not deny that there are many anglers who have carried sunk fly and even worm casting to a high degree of specialisation and refinement; yet it seems to me— nay, more than that, it is a positive conviction with me—that no manner of sunk fly or worm or bait casting bears any sort of favourable comparison to the manner of the dry fly. I know that in this country, at least, the dry fly man is accused by his sunk fly fellows of being affected, dogmatic, fanatic. Yet it is not so. The dry fly man has passed through all of the stages of the angler's life, from the cane pole and the drop-line to the split bamboo and the fur-and-feather counterfeit of the midge fly. He has experienced throes of delight each time he advanced from the lower to the higher grade of angler. I insist that I do not make my words too strong when I say that in all of angling there is no greater delight than that which comes to the dry fly angler who simulates a hatch of flies, and entices to the surface of the water a fish lying hidden, unseen, in the stronghold of his own selection. Let him who doubts put aside his prejudice long enough to give the premier method fair trial, and soon he will be found applying for the highest degree of the cult—"dry fly man."

CHAPTER VIII

A FEW PATTERNS OF FLIES

THE literature devoted to the subject of the artificial fly is very extensive and informing, and it is not my intention to add thereto except for the purpose of describing a few flies that I use in my own fishing. The tackle shops offer almost countless patterns of flies of varied hues and forms, and anglers can indulge their individual tastes by choosing sizes, colours, and shapes to suit their fancies. I have never attempted to compute the number of artificial flies listed in the dealers' catalogues and described in the works of angling writers, but I think it must run into the hundreds. There is, however, a growing tendency toward restriction in the number of special patterns used in actual fishing, and in my own fishing I have reduced this number to a very small one.

It is doubtless true that the fly fisher derives no small part of his pleasure from the act of selecting and purchasing flies. It is within the experience of every fly fisher, I think, that, under the influence of the memory of a certain fish taken on a particular pattern of fly, he includes a dozen or two of the sort in his next purchase. Perhaps the fly is a nondescript that he may never again find successful, but, nevertheless, he adds it to his store. Angling friends recommend their patterns to him, or some special flies they found taking under certain circumstances or over particular streams, and these, too, he buys and puts away. Maybe he may never use one of them, and in the end he comes, perhaps, to feel, as does the philatelist, great pleasure in the possession of a worthy collection: he has the pride of ownership, but no thought of putting his treasures to use. Of course, there can be no reasonable objection to fly collecting, and I can see how it may become as fascinating an employment as stamp or coin collecting.

Assuming that the angler is a believer in close imitation, he will, of course, be content only when he has all of the patterns which have been created by the votaries of the theory; but if he should be inclined to agree with me—that a great part of the imitation must be produced by the angler himself while actually fishing the stream—he will find that about ten patterns will suffice under nearly all circumstances.

I give the dressings of eight patterns, although I rarely use over six. If I were compelled to do so, I could get along very well with one—the Whirling Dun. Fishing the Brodhead throughout the month of July, I used this fly exclusively, and took fish every day except two. On three separate occasions I used a different fly—at one time a Pink Lady, at another a Mole, and at still another a Silver Sedge. On each occasion I took one fish with the selected fly, after which I went back to the Whirling Dun, and continued my fishing. I killed one or two fish each day, the average for the month being very close to a pound and a half. I returned many fish to the water, and these averaged over ten inches. Some days the fish were feeding, and some days they were not. There was apparently little difference in the taking effect of the fly, except that it was taken readily when it was delivered properly, and never when it was not.

No matter how great the faith an angler has in a single pattern, it will naturally be very difficult for him to confine himself to its exclusive use. So much of his sport depends upon its delightful uncertainty, that if he does confine himself to the use of the single pattern, he will, of a consequence, be denied the pleasure of congratulating himself upon the acumen he has shown by the selection of the fly which is taken, after the favourite has been refused.

With the exception of the Pink Lady, the flies described are all standard patterns—tied, however, according to my own preference. Anglers who wish a more varied choice, one that includes one or two fancies, may add to the list a Wickham's Fancy and, for use when the fish are smutting, a small black gnat tied with a glossy black hackle and no wings—a variety that will often prove very effective when the fish are feeding in that manner. A Marlow Buzz may be included for use on windy days when the larger land insects are blown upon the water.

The flies commonly used by me, with their dressings, are as follows:

WHIRLING DUN (BLUE)

Wings.—Starling or duck, medium light.
Body. —Water-rat or mole fur; two turns of flat gold tinsel around hook at end of body.
Legs. —Glossy ginger or light brown cock's hackle.
Tail. —Three whisks of same.

PALE EVENING DUN (WATERY DUN)

Wings.—Light starling.
Body. —Lemon mohair lightly dressed.
Legs. —Glossy barred Plymouth Rock cock's hackle.
Tail. —Two or three whisks of same.

PINK LADY

Wings.—Medium starling or duck.
Body. —Pale pink floss ribbed with flat gold tinsel.
Legs. —Ginger or light reddish-brown hackle.
Tail. —Three whisks of same.

GOLD-RIBBED HARE'S EAR

Wings.—Medium starling or duck.
Body. —Hare's fur ribbed with flat gold tinsel body,
             not too heavy.
Legs. —Hare's fur tied on with silk.
Tail. —Two or three rather long whisks, grey mallard.

FLIGHT'S FANCY

Wings.—Light starling or duck.
Body. —Pale yellow floss ribbed with flat gold tinsel.
Legs. —Ginger hackle.
Tail. —Two or three whisks of same.
     The body of this fly will turn green when wet,
which is nothing against it, however.

SILVER SEDGE

Wings.—Rather dark starling.
Body. —White floss ribbed with flat silver tinsel.
Legs. —Pale ginger hackle.
Tail. —Two or three whisks of same.
     The body of this fly will turn a greyish-blue
when wet, but the change does not affect its taking
qualities.

WILLOW

Wings.—None.
Body. —Light blue fur, mole or fox, ribbed with light
        yellow silk.
Legs. —Glossy white or transparent hackle.
Tail. —Two whisks of same.

MOLE

Wings.—Medium starling or duck.
Body. —Light mole fur lightly dressed and tightly wound.
Legs. —Purplish-brown (dyed), hackle tied palmer-wise.
Tail. —Three or four whisks of same.
        The standard pattern of this fly is tied with light
brown woodcock wings.

It is advisable that each of the patterns be tied on hooks of different sizes—Nos. 10, 12, 14, and 16 will suffice—because the size of the fly is often important, particularly when the water is very low and clear.

If a greater aid is required in floating the fly (barring the use of paraffin) other than a stiff hackle at the shoulder, I would recommend that a short-fibred hackle be tied on at the shoulder and carried around and down the body to the tail, the fibres being cut off close to the body after tying. The effect of this dressing will be to make the fly float better, particularly after some use, and after the points of the longer shoulder hackles have been submerged.

The short fibres along the body, by intercepting some light and permitting some to pass through, will help to produce the effect of transparency or translucency of the natural insect, which effect would be particularly noticeable upon flies where quill is used for the body. The use of this hackle can be dispensed with in the case of those flies where fur or mohair is used for the body—a few fibres picked out with a needle producing much the same appearance and effect.

It may be the experience of other anglers who have experimented with the artificial fly in attempts to produce one that would cock readily and maintain a good balance on the water, that one tied with the wings leaning rather more forward than is the present practice, offers the nearest solution to these difficulties. My own experience is that flies tied in this manner sit beautifully upon the water, but I cannot say that they cock any more frequently than those tied with upright wings. I would suggest that the angler tie a few flies with the wings tilted forward at an angle of about 120°, and try them. If nothing else is accomplished, the experiment may lead to a development in the form of the fly which will enable us all to some day take the one "big fish."